WO - 2 - 4390

PLAYS BY AUGUST STRINDBERG
PUBLISHED BY CHARLES SCRIBNER'S SONS

THERE ARE CRIMES AND CRIMES
75 cents *net*; postage extra

PLAYS: The Dream Play, The Link, The Dance of
Death—Part I and Part II
$1.50 *net*; postage extra

# THERE ARE
# CRIMES AND CRIMES

# THERE ARE
# CRIMES AND CRIMES
## A COMEDY

BY

## AUGUST STRINDBERG

TRANSLATED FROM THE SWEDISH WITH AN INTRODUCTION BY

## EDWIN BJÖRKMAN

AUTHORIZED EDITION

NEW YORK
CHARLES SCRIBNER'S SONS
1912

# INTRODUCTION

# INTRODUCTION

STRINDBERG was fifty years old when he wrote "There Are Crimes and Crimes." In the same year, 1899, he produced three of his finest historical dramas: "The Saga of the Folkungs," "Gustavus Vasa," and "Eric XIV." Just before, he had finished "Advent," which he described as "A Mystery," and which was published together with "There Are Crimes and Crimes" under the common title of "In a Higher Court." Back of these dramas lay his strange confessional works, "Inferno" and "Legends," and the first two parts of his autobiographical dream-play, "Toward Damascus"—all of which were finished between May, 1897, and some time in the latter part of 1898. And back of these again lay that period of mental crisis, when, at Paris, in 1895 and 1896, he strove to make gold by the transmutation of baser metals, while at the same time his spirit was travelling through all the seven hells in its search for the heaven promised by the great mystics of the past.

"There Are Crimes and Crimes" may, in fact, be regarded as his first definite step beyond that crisis, of which the preceding works were at once the record and closing chord. When, in 1909, he issued "The Author," being a long withheld fourth part of his first autobiographical series, "The Bondwoman's Son," he prefixed to it an analytical summary of the entire body of his work. Opposite the works from 1897–8 appears in this summary the following passage: "The great crisis at the age of fifty; revolutions in the life of the soul, desert wanderings, Swedenborgian Heavens and Hells." But concerning "There Are Crimes and Crimes" and the three historical dramas from the same year he writes triumphantly: "Light after darkness; new productivity, with recovered Faith, Hope and Love—and with full, rock-firm Certitude."

In its German version the play is named "Rausch," or "Intoxication," which indicates the part played by the champagne in the plunge of *Maurice* from the pinnacles of success to the depths of misfortune.  Strindberg has more and more come to see that a moderation verging closely on asceticism is wise for most men and essential to the man of genius who wants to fulfil his divine mission.  And he does not scorn to press home even this comparatively humble lesson with the naïve directness and fiery zeal which form such conspicuous features of all his work.

But in the title which bound it to "Advent" at their joint publication we have a better clue to what the author himself undoubtedly regards as the most important element of his work—its religious tendency.  The "higher court," in which are tried the crimes of *Maurice*, *Adolphe*, and *Henriette*, is, of course, the highest one that man can imagine. And the crimes of which they have all become guilty are those which, as *Adolphe* remarks, "are not mentioned in the criminal code"—in a word, crimes against the spirit, against the impalpable power that moves us, against God.  The play, seen in this light, pictures a deep-reaching spiritual change, leading us step by step from the soul adrift on the waters of life to the state where it is definitely oriented and impelled.

There are two distinct currents discernible in this dramatic revelation of progress from spiritual chaos to spiritual order —for to order the play must be said to lead, and progress is implied in its onward movement, if there be anything at all in our growing modern conviction that *any* vital faith is better than none at all.  One of the currents in question refers to the means rather than the end, to the road rather than the goal. It brings us back to those uncanny soul-adventures by which Strindberg himself won his way to the "full, rock-firm Certitude" of which the play in its entirety is the first tangible expression. The elements entering into this current are not only mystical, but occult. They are derived in part from Swedenborg, and in part from that picturesque French dreamer who signs himself "Sar Péladan"; but mostly they have sprung out of Strindberg's own experiences in moments of abnormal tension.

What happened, or seemed to happen, to himself at Paris in 1895, and what he later described with such bewildering exactitude in his "Inferno" and "Legends," all this is here presented in dramatic form, but a little toned down, both to suit the needs of the stage and the calmer mood of the author. Coincidence is law. It is the finger-point of Providence, the signal to man that he must beware. Mystery is the gospel: the secret knitting of man to man, of fact to fact, deep beneath the surface of visible and audible existence. Few writers could take us into such a realm of probable impossibilities and possible improbabilities without losing all claim to serious consideration. If Strindberg has thus ventured to our gain and no loss of his own, his success can be explained only by the presence in the play of that second, parallel current of thought and feeling.

This deeper current is as simple as the one nearer the surface is fantastic. It is the manifestation of that "rock-firm Certitude" to which I have already referred. And nothing will bring us nearer to it than Strindberg's own confession of faith, given in his "Speeches to the Swedish Nation" two years ago. In that pamphlet there is a chapter headed "Religion," in which occurs this passage: "Since 1896 I have been calling myself a Christian. I am not a Catholic, and have never been, but during a stay of seven years in Catholic countries and among Catholic relatives, I discovered that the difference between Catholic and Protestant tenets is either none at all, or else wholly superficial, and that the division which once occurred was merely political or else concerned with theological problems not fundamentally germane to the religion itself. A registered Protestant I am and will remain, but I can hardly be called orthodox or evangelistic, but come nearest to being a Swedenborgian. I use my Bible Christianity internally and privately to tame my somewhat decivilized nature—decivilised by that veterinary philosophy and animal science (Darwinism) in which, as student at the university, I was reared. And I assure my fellow-beings that they have no right to complain because, according to my ability, I practise the Christian teachings. For only through religion, or the hope of something better, and the recognition of the innermost meaning of life as that of an ordeal, a school, or perhaps a penitentiary, will it be possible to bear the burden of life with sufficient resignation."

Here, as alsewhere, it is made patent that Strindberg's religiosity always, on closer analysis, reduces itself to morality. At bottom he is first and last, and has always been, a moralist—a man passionately craving to know what is *right* and to do it. During the middle, naturalistic period of his creative career, this fundamental tendency was in part obscured, and he engaged in the game of intellectual curiosity known as "truth for truth's own sake." One of the chief marks of his final and mystical period is his greater courage to "be himself" in this respect—and this means necessarily a return, or an advance, to a position which the late William James undoubtedly would have acknowledged as "pragmatic." To combat the assertion of over-developed individualism that we are ends in ourselves, that we have certain inalienable personal "rights" to pleasure and happiness merely because we happen to appear here in human shape, this is one of Strindberg's most ardent aims in all his later works.

As to the higher and more inclusive object to which our lives must be held subservient, he is not dogmatic. It may be another life. He calls it God. And the code of service he finds in the tenets of all the Christian churches, but principally in the Commandments. The plain and primitive virtues, the faith that implies little more than square dealing between man and man—these figure foremost in Strindberg's ideals. In an age of supreme self-seeking like ours, such an outlook would seem to have small chance of popularity, but that it embodies just what the time most needs is, perhaps, made evident by the reception which the public almost invariably grants "There Are Crimes and Crimes" when it is staged.

With all its apparent disregard of what is commonly called realism, and with its occasional, but quite unblushing, use of methods generally held superseded—such as the casual introduction of characters at whatever moment they happen to be needed on the stage—it has, from the start, been among the most frequently played and most enthusiastically received of Strindberg's later dramas. At Stockholm it was first taken up by the Royal Dramatic Theatre, and was later seen on the tiny stage of the Intimate Theatre, then devoted exclusively to Strindberg's works. It was one of the earliest plays staged by Reinhardt while he was still experimenting with his Little Theatre at Berlin, and it has also been given in numerous German cities, as well as in Vienna.

Concerning my own version of the play I wish to add a word of explanation. Strindberg has laid the scene in Paris. Not only the scenery, but the people and the circumstances are French. Yet he has made no attempt whatever to make the dialogue reflect French manners of speaking or ways of thinking. As he has given it to us, the play is French only in its most superficial aspect, in its setting—and this setting he has chosen simply because he needed a certain machinery offered him by the Catholic, but not by the Protestant, churches. The rest of the play is purely human in its note and wholly universal in its spirit. For this reason I have retained the French names and titles, but have otherwise striven to bring everything as close as possible to our own modes of expression. Should apparent incongruities result from this manner of treatment, I think they will disappear if only the reader will try to remember that the characters of the play move in an existence cunningly woven by the author out of scraps of ephemeral reality in order that he may show us the mirage of a more enduring one.

# THERE ARE
# CRIMES AND CRIMES

## A COMEDY

## 1899

# CHARACTERS

MAURICE, *a playwright*
JEANNE, *his mistress*
MARION, *their daughter, five years old*
ADOLPHE, *a painter*
HENRIETTE, *his mistress*
EMILE, *a workman, brother of Jeanne*
MADAME CATHERINE
THE ABBÉ
A WATCHMAN
A HEAD WAITER
A COMMISSAIRE
TWO DETECTIVES
A WAITER
A GUARD
A SERVANT GIRL

*All the scenes are laid in Paris*

# THERE ARE
# CRIMES AND CRIMES

## ACT I

### FIRST SCENE

*The upper avenue of cypresses in the Montparnasse Cemetery
at Paris. The background shows mortuary chapels, stone
crosses on which are inscribed "O Crux! Ave Spes Unica!"
and the ruins of a wind-mill covered with ivy.*

*A well-dressed woman in widow's weeds is kneeling and mutter-
ing prayers in front of a grave decorated with flowers.*

JEANNE *is walking back and forth as if expecting somebody.*

MARION *is playing with some withered flowers picked from a
rubbish heap on the ground.*

*The* ABBÉ *is reading his breviary while walking along the
further end of the avenue.*

WATCHMAN. [*Enters and goes up to* JEANNE] Look here,
this is no playground.

JEANNE. [*Submissively*] I am only waiting for somebody
who'll soon be here——

WATCHMAN. All right, but you're not allowed to pick any
flowers.

JEANNE. [*To* MARION] Drop the flowers, dear.

ABBÉ. [*Comes forward and is saluted by the* WATCHMAN]
Can't the child play with the flowers that have been thrown
away?

WATCHMAN. The regulations don't permit anybody to
touch even the flowers that have been thrown away, because

11

it's believed they may spread infection—which I don't know if it's true.

ABBÉ. [*To* MARION] In that case we have to obey, of course. What's your name, my little girl?

MARION. My name is Marion.

ABBÉ. And who is your father?

> MARION *begins to bite one of her fingers and does not answer.*

ABBÉ. Pardon my question, madame. I had no intention —I was just talking to keep the little one quiet.

> *The* WATCHMAN *has gone out.*

JEANNE. I understood it, Reverend Father, and I wish you would say something to quiet me also. I feel very much disturbed after having waited here two hours.

ABBÉ. Two hours—for him! How these human beings torture each other! O Crux! Ave spes unica!

JEANNE. What do they mean, those words you read all around here?

ABBÉ. They mean: O cross, our only hope!

JEANNE. Is it the only one?

ABBÉ. The only certain one.

JEANNE. I shall soon believe that you are right, Father.

ABBÉ. May I ask why?

JEANNE. You have already guessed it. When he lets the woman and the child wait two hours in a cemetery, then the end is not far off.

ABBÉ. And when he has left you, what then?

JEANNE. Then we have to go into the river.

ABBÉ. Oh, no, no!

JEANNE. Yes, yes!

MARION. Mamma, I want to go home, for I am hungry.

JEANNE. Just a little longer, dear, and we'll go home.

ABBÉ. Woe unto those who call evil good and good evil.

JEANNE. What is that woman doing at the grave over there?

ABBÉ. She seems to be talking to the dead.

JEANNE. But you cannot do that?

ABBÉ. She seems to know how.

JEANNE. This would mean that the end of life is not the end of our misery?

ABBÉ. And you don't know it?

JEANNE. Where can I find out?

ABBÉ. Hm! The next time you feel as if you wanted to learn about this well-known matter, you can look me up in Our Lady's Chapel at the Church of St. Germain— Here comes the one you are waiting for, I guess.

JEANNE. [*Embarrassed*] No, he is not the one, but I know him.

ABBÉ. [*To* MARION] Good-bye, little Marion! May God take care of you! [*Kisses the child and goes out*] At St. Germain des Prés.

EMILE. [*Enters*] Good morning, sister. What are you doing here?

JEANNE. I am waiting for Maurice.

EMILE. Then I guess you'll have a lot of waiting to do, for I saw him on the boulevard an hour ago, taking breakfast with some friends. [*Kissing the child*] Good morning, Marion.

JEANNE. Ladies also?

EMILE. Of course. But that doesn't mean anything. He writes plays, and his latest one has its first performance to-night. I suppose he had with him some of the actresses.

JEANNE. Did he recognise you?

EMILE. No, he doesn't know who I am, and it is just as well. I know my place as a workman, and I don't care for any condescension from those that are above me.

JEANNE. But if he leaves us without anything to live on?

EMILE. Well, you see, when it gets that far, then I suppose I shall have to introduce myself. But you don't expect anything of the kind, do you—seeing that he is fond of you and very much attached to the child?

JEANNE. I don't know, but I have a feeling that something dreadful is in store for me.

EMILE. Has he promised to marry you?

JEANNE. No, not promised exactly, but he has held out hopes.

EMILE. Hopes, yes! Do you remember my words at the start: don't hope for anything, for those above us don't marry downward.

JEANNE. But such things have happened.

EMILE. Yes, they have happened. But would you feel at home in his world? I can't believe it, for you wouldn't even understand what they were talking of. Now and then I take my meals where he is eating—out in the kitchen is my place, of course—and I don't make out a word of what they say.

JEANNE. So you take your meals at that place?

EMILE. Yes, in the kitchen.

JEANNE. And think of it, he has never asked me to come with him.

EMILE. Well, that's rather to his credit, and it shows he has some respect for the mother of his child. The women over there are a queer lot.

JEANNE. Is that so?

EMILE. But Maurice never pays any attention to the women. There is something *square* about that fellow.

JEANNE. That's what I feel about him, too, but as soon as there is a woman in it, a man isn't himself any longer.

EMILE. [*Smiling*] You don't tell me! But listen: are you hard up for money?

JEANNE. No, nothing of that kind.

EMILE. Well, then the worst hasn't come yet— Look! Over there! There he comes. And I'll leave you. Good-bye, little girl.

JEANNE. Is he coming? Yes, that's him.

EMILE. Don't make him mad now—with your jealousy, Jeanne!              [*Goes out.*

JEANNE. No, I won't.

     MAURICE *enters.*

MARION. [*Runs up to him and is lifted up into his arms*] Papa, papa!

MAURICE. My little girl! [*Greets* JEANNE] Can you forgive me, Jeanne, that I have kept you waiting so long?

JEANNE. Of course I can.

MAURICE. But say it in such a way that I can hear that you are forgiving me.

JEANNE. Come here and let me whisper it to you.

     MAURICE *goes up close to her.*

     JEANNE *kisses him on the cheek.*

MAURICE. I didn't hear.

     JEANNE *kisses him on the mouth.*

MAURICE. Now I heard! Well—you know, I suppose that this is the day that will settle my fate? My play is on for to-night, and there is every chance that it will succeed—or fail.

JEANNE. I'll make sure of success by praying for you.

MAURICE. Thank you. If it doesn't help, it can at least do no harm— Look over there, down there in the valley, where the haze is thickest: there lies Paris. To-day Paris doesn't know who Maurice is, but it is going to know within twenty-four hours. The haze, which has kept me obscured for thirty years, will vanish before my breath, and I shall become visible, I shall assume definite shape and begin to be somebody. My enemies—which means all who would like to do what I have done—will be writhing in pains that shall be my pleasures, for they will be suffering all that I have suffered.

JEANNE. Don't talk that way, don't!

MAURICE. But that's the way it is.

JEANNE. Yes, but don't speak of it—  And then?

MAURICE. Then we are on firm ground, and then you and Marion will bear the name I have made famous.

JEANNE. You love me then?

MAURICE. I love both of you, equally much, or perhaps Marion a little more.

JEANNE. I am glad of it, for you can grow tired of me, but not of her.

MAURICE. Have you no confidence in my feelings toward you?

JEANNE. I don't know, but I am, afraid of something, afraid of something terrible——

MAURICE. You are tired out and depressed by your long wait, which once more I ask you to forgive.   What have you to be afraid of?

JEANNE. The unexpected: that which you may foresee without having any particular reason to do so.

MAURICE. But I foresee only success, and I have particular reasons for doing so: the keen instincts of the management and their knowledge of the public, not to speak of their personal acquaintance with the critics.   So now you must be in good spirits——

JEANNE. I can't, I can't!  Do you know, there was an Abbé here a while ago, who talked so beautifully to us.   My faith—which you haven't destroyed, but just covered up, as when you put chalk on a window to clean it—I couldn't lay hold on it for that reason, but this old man just passed his hand over the chalk, and the light came through, and it was possible again to see that the people within were at home— To-night I will pray for you at St. Germain.

MAURICE. Now I am getting scared.

JEANNE. Fear of God is the beginning of wisdom.

MAURICE. God? What is that? Who is he?

JEANNE. It was he who gave joy to your youth and strength to your manhood. And it is he who will carry us through the terrors that lie ahead of us.

MAURICE. What is lying ahead of us? What do you know? Where have you learned of this? This thing that I don't know?

JEANNE. I can't tell. I have dreamt nothing, seen nothing, heard nothing. But during these two dreadful hours I have experienced such an infinity of pain that I am ready for the worst.

MARION. Now I want to go home, mamma, for I am hungry.

MAURICE. Yes, you'll go home now, my little darling.

[*Takes her into his arms.*

MARION. [*Shrinking*] Oh, you hurt me, papa!

JEANNE. Yes, we must get home for dinner. Good-bye then, Maurice. And good luck to you!

MAURICE. [*To* MARION] How did I hurt you? Doesn't my little girl know that I always want to be nice to her?

MARION. If you are nice, you'll come home with us.

MAURICE. [*To* JEANNE] When I hear the child talk like that, you know, I feel as if I ought to do what she says. But then reason and duty protest— Good-bye, my dear little girl! [*He kisses the child, who puts her arms around his neck.*

JEANNE. When do we meet again?

MAURICE. We'll meet to-morrow, dear. And then we'll never part again.

JEANNE. [*Embraces him*] Never, never to part again! [*She

*makes the sign of the cross on his forehead*] May God protect you!

MAURICE. [*Moved against his own will*] My dear, beloved Jeanne!

> JEANNE *and* MARION *go toward the right;* MAURICE *toward the left. Both turn around simultaneously and throw kisses at each other.*

MAURICE. [*Comes back*] Jeanne, I am ashamed of myself. I am always forgetting you, and you are the last one to remind me of it. Here are the tickets for to-night.

JEANNE. Thank you, dear, but—you have to take up your post of duty alone, and so I have to take up mine—with Marion.

MAURICE. Your wisdom is as great as the goodness of your heart. Yes, I am sure no other woman would have sacrificed a pleasure to serve her husband— I must have my hands free to-night, and there is no place for women and children on the battle-field—and this you understood!

JEANNE. Don't think too highly of a poor woman like myself, and then you'll have no illusions to lose. And now you'll see that I can be as forgetful as you—I have bought you a tie and a pair of gloves which I thought you might wear for my sake on your day of honour.

MAURICE. [*Kissing her hand*] Thank you, dear.

JEANNE. And then, Maurice, don't forget to have your hair fixed, as you do all the time. I want you to be good-looking, so that others will like you too.

MAURICE. There is no jealousy in *you!*

JEANNE. Don't mention that word, for evil thoughts spring from it.

MAURICE. Just now I feel as if I could give up this evening's victory—for I am going to win——

JEANNE. Hush, hush!

MAURICE. And go home with you instead.

JEANNE. But you mustn't do that! Go now: your destiny is waiting for you.

MAURICE. Good-bye then! And may that happen which must happen! [*Goes out.*

JEANNE. [*Alone with* MARION] O Crux! Ave spes unica!

*Curtain.*

### SECOND SCENE

*The Crêmerie. On the right stands a buffet, on which are placed an aquarium with goldfish and dishes containing vegetables, fruit, preserves, etc. In the background is a door leading to the kitchen, where workmen are taking their meals. At the other end of the kitchen can be seen a door leading out to a garden. On the left, in the background, stands a counter on a raised platform, and back of it are shelves containing all sorts of bottles. On the right, a long table with a marble top is placed along the wall, and another table is placed parallel to the first further out on the floor. Straw-bottomed chairs stand around the tables. The walls are covered with oil-paintings.*

MME. CATHERINE *is sitting at the counter.*

MAURICE *stands leaning against it. He has his hat on and is smoking a cigarette.*

MME. CATHERINE. So it's to-night the great event comes off, Monsieur Maurice?

MAURICE. Yes, to-night.

MME. CATHERINE. Do you feel upset?

MAURICE. Cool as a cucumber.

MME. CATHERINE. Well, I wish you luck anyhow, and you

have deserved it, Monsieur Maurice, after having had to fight against such difficulties as yours.

MAURICE. Thank you, Madame Catherine. You have been very kind to me, and without your help I should probably have been down and out by this time.

MME. CATHERINE. Don't let us talk of that now. I help along where I see hard work and the right kind of will, but I don't want to be exploited— Can we trust you to come back here after the play and let us drink a glass with you?

MAURICE. Yes, you can—of course, you can, as I have already promised you.

HENRIETTE *enters from the right.*

MAURICE *turns around, raises his hat, and stares at* HENRIETTE, *who looks him over carefully.*

HENRIETTE. Monsieur Adolphe is not here yet?

MME. CATHERINE. No, madame. But he'll soon be here now. Won't you sit down?

HENRIETTE. No, thank you, I'll rather wait for him outside. [*Goes out.*

MAURICE. Who—was—that?

MME. CATHERINE. Why, that's Monsieur Adolphe's friend.

MAURICE. Was—that—her?

MME. CATHERINE. Have you never seen her before?

MAURICE. No, he has been hiding her from me, just as if he was afraid I might take her away from him.

MME. CATHERINE. Ha-ha!— Well, how did you think she looked?

MAURICE. How she looked? Let me see: I can't tell— I didn't see her, for it was as if she had rushed straight into my arms at once and come so close to me that I couldn't make out her features at all. And she left her impression on the air behind her. I can still see her standing there. [*He goes toward the door and makes a gesture as if putting his arm around somebody*] Whew! [*He makes a gesture as if he had pricked his finger*] There are pins in her waist.　She is of the kind that stings!

MME. CATHERINE. Oh, you are crazy, you with your ladies!

MAURICE. Yes, it's craziness, that's what it is.　But do you know, Madame Catherine, I am going before she comes back, or else, or else—　Oh, that woman is horrible!

MME. CATHERINE. Are you afraid?

MAURICE. Yes, I am afraid for myself, and also for some others.

MME. CATHERINE. Well, go then.

MAURICE. She seemed to suck herself out through the door, and in her wake rose a little whirlwind that dragged me along—　Yes, you may laugh, but can't you see that the palm over there on the buffet is still shaking?　She's the very devil of a woman!

MME. CATHERINE. Oh, get out of here, man, before you lose all your reason.

MAURICE. I want to go, but I cannot—　Do you believe in fate, Madame Catherine?

MME. CATHERINE. No, I believe in a good God, who protects us against evil powers if we ask Him in the right way.

MAURICE. So there are evil powers after all!　I think I can hear them in the hallway now.

MME. CATHERINE. Yes, her clothes rustle as when the clerk tears off a piece of linen for you.　Get away now— through the kitchen.

　　　MAURICE *rushes toward the kitchen door, where he bumps
　　　　　into* EMILE.

EMILE. I beg your pardon.　　　[*He retires the way he came.*

ADOLPHE. [*Comes in first; after him* HENRIETTE] Why, there's Maurice.　How are you?　Let me introduce this lady

here to my oldest and best friend.   Mademoiselle Henriette—
Monsieur Maurice.

MAURICE. [*Saluting stiffly*] Pleased to meet you.

HENRIETTE. We have seen each other before.

ADOLPHE. Is that so?   When, if I may ask?

MAURICE. A moment ago.   Right here.

ADOLPHE. O-oh!—  But now you must stay and have a
chat with us.

MAURICE. [*After a glance at* MME. CATHERINE] If I only
had time.

ADOLPHE. Take the time.   And we won't be sitting here
very long.

HENRIETTE. I won't interrupt, if you have to talk business.

MAURICE. The only business we have is so bad that we
don't want to talk of it.

HENRIETTE. Then we'll talk of something else. [*Takes the
hat away from* MAURICE *and hangs it up*] Now be nice, and
let me become acquainted with the great author.

    MME. CATHERINE *signals to* MAURICE, *who doesn't no-*
       *tice her.*

ADOLPHE. That's right, Henriette, you take charge of him.
        [*They seat themselves at one of the tables.*

HENRIETTE. [*To* MAURICE] You certainly have a good
friend in Adolphe, Monsieur Maurice.  He never talks of
anything but you, and in such a way that I feel myself
rather thrown in the background.

ADOLPHE. You don't say so!   Well, Henriette on her side
never leaves me in peace about you, Maurice.   She has read
your works, and she is always wanting to know where you
got this and where that.   She has been questioning me about
your looks, your age, your tastes.   I have, in a word, had
you for breakfast, dinner, and supper.   It has almost seemed
as if the three of us were living together.

MAURICE. [*To* HENRIETTE] Heavens, why didn't you come over here and have a look at this wonder of wonders? Then your curiosity could have been satisfied in a trice.

HENRIETTE. Adolphe didn't want it.

ADOLPHE *looks embarrassed*.

HENRIETTE. Not that he was jealous——

MAURICE. And why should he be, when he knows that my feelings are tied up elsewhere?

HENRIETTE. Perhaps he didn't trust the stability of your feelings.

MAURICE. I can't understand that, seeing that I am notorious for my constancy.

ADOLPHE. Well, it wasn't that——

HENRIETTE. [*Interrupting him*] Perhaps that is because you have not faced the fiery ordeal——

ADOLPHE. Oh, you don't know——

HENRIETTE. [*Interrupting*]—for the world has not yet beheld a faithful man.

MAURICE. Then it's going to behold one.

HENRIETTE. Where?

MAURICE. Here.

HENRIETTE *laughs*.

ADOLPHE. Well, that's going it——

HENRIETTE. [*Interrupting him and directing herself continuously to* MAURICE] Do you think I ever trust my dear Adolphe more than a month at a time?

MAURICE. I have no right to question your lack of confidence, but I can guarantee that Adolphe is faithful.

HENRIETTE. You don't need to do so—my tongue is just running away with me, and I have to take back a lot—not only for fear of feeling less generous than you, but because it is the truth. It is a bad habit I have of only seeing the ugly side of things, and I keep it up although I know better. But if I had a chance to be with you two for some time, then your company would make me good once more. Pardon me, Adolphe!          [*She puts her hand against his cheek.*

ADOLPHE. You are always wrong in your talk and right in your actions. What you really think—that I don't know.

HENRIETTE. Who does know that kind of thing?

MAURICE. Well, if we had to answer for our thoughts, who could then clear himself?

HENRIETTE. Do you also have evil thoughts?

MAURICE. Certainly; just as I commit the worst kind of cruelties in my dreams.

HENRIETTE. Oh, when you are dreaming, of course— Just think of it—  No, I am ashamed of telling——

MAURICE. Go on, go on!

HENRIETTE. Last night I dreamt that I was coolly dissecting the muscles on Adolphe's breast—you see, I am a sculptor —and he, with his usual kindness, made no resistance, but helped me instead with the worst places, as he knows more anatomy than I.

MAURICE. Was he dead?

HENRIETTE. No, he was living.

MAURICE. But that's horrible! And didn't it make *you* suffer?

HENRIETTE. Not at all, and that astonished me most, for I am rather sensitive to other people's sufferings. Isn't that so, Adolphe?

ADOLPHE. That's right. Rather abnormally so, in fact, and not the least when animals are concerned.

MAURICE. And I, on the other hand, am rather callous toward the sufferings both of myself and others.

ADOLPHE. Now he is not telling the truth about himself. Or what do you say, Madame Catherine?

MME. CATHERINE. I don't know of anybody with a softer

heart than Monsieur Maurice.   He came near calling in the
police because I didn't give the goldfish fresh water—those
over there on the buffet.   Just look at them: it is as if they
could hear what I am saying.

MAURICE. Yes, here we are making ourselves out as white
as angels, and yet we are, taking it all in all, capable of any
kind of polite atrocity the moment glory, gold, or women are
concerned—   So you are a sculptor, Mademoiselle Henriette?

HENRIETTE. A bit of one.   Enough to do a bust.   And to
do one of you—which has long been my cherished dream—I
hold myself quite capable.

MAURICE. Go ahead!   That dream at least need not be
long in coming true.

HENRIETTE. But I don't want to fix your features in my
mind until this evening's success is over.   Not until then
will you have become what you should be.

MAURICE. How sure you are of victory!

HENRIETTE. Yes, it is written on your face that you are
going to win this battle, and I think you must feel that
yourself.

MAURICE. Why do you think so?

HENRIETTE. Because I can feel it.   This morning I was
ill, you know, and now I am well.

ADOLPHE *begins to look depressed.*

MAURICE. [*Embarrassed*] Listen, I have a single ticket left
—only one.   I place it at your disposal, Adolphe.

ADOLPHE. Thank you, but I surrender it to Henriette.

HENRIETTE. But that wouldn't do?

ADOLPHE. Why not?   And I never go to the theatre anyhow, as I cannot stand the  heat.

HENRIETTE. But you will come and take us home at least
after the show is over.

ADOLPHE. If you insist on it. Otherwise Maurice has to come back here, where we shall all be waiting for him.

MAURICE. You can just as well take the trouble of meeting us. In fact, I ask, I beg you to do so— And if you don't want to wait outside the theatre, you can meet us at the Auberge des Adrets— That's settled then, isn't it?

ADOLPHE. Wait a little. You have a way of settling things to suit yourself, before other people have a chance to consider them.

MAURICE. What is there to consider—whether you are to see your lady home or not?

ADOLPHE. You never know what may be involved in a simple act like that, but I have a sort of premonition.

HENRIETTE. Hush, hush, hush! Don't talk of spooks while the sun is shining. Let him come or not, as it pleases him. We can always find our way back here.

ADOLPHE. [Rising] Well, now I have to leave you—model, you know. Good-bye, both of you. And good luck to you, Maurice. To-morrow you will be out on the right side. Good-bye, Henriette.

HENRIETTE. Do you really have to go?

ADOLPHE. I must.

MAURICE. Good-bye then. We'll meet later.

Adolphe goes out, saluting MME. CATHERINE in passing.

HENRIETTE. Think of it, that we should meet at last!

MAURICE. Do you find anything remarkable in that?

HENRIETTE. It looks as if it had to happen, for Adolphe has done his best to prevent it.

MAURICE. Has he?

HENRIETTE. Oh, you must have noticed it.

MAURICE. I have noticed it, but why should you mention it?

HENRIETTE. I had to.

MAURICE. No, and I don't have to tell you that I wanted to run away through the kitchen in order to avoid meeting you and was stopped by a guest who closed the door in front of me.

HENRIETTE. Why do you tell me about it now?

MAURICE. I don't know.

MME. CATHERINE *upsets a number of glasses and bottles.*

MAURICE. That's all right, Madame Catherine. There's nothing to be afraid of.

HENRIETTE. Was that meant as a signal or a warning?

MAURICE. Probably both.

HENRIETTE. Do they take me for a locomotive that has to have flagmen ahead of it?

MAURICE. And switchmen! The danger is always greatest at the switches.

HENRIETTE. How nasty you can be!

MME. CATHERINE. Monsieur Maurice isn't nasty at all. So far nobody has been kinder than he to those that love him and trust in him.

MAURICE. Sh, sh, sh!

HENRIETTE. [*To* MAURICE] The old lady is rather impertinent.

MAURICE. We can walk over to the boulevard, if you care to do so.

HENRIETTE. With pleasure. This is not the place for me. I can just feel their hatred clawing at me.          [*Goes out.*

MAURICE. [*Starts after her*] Good-bye, Madame Catherine.

MME. CATHERINE. A moment! May I speak a word to you, Monsieur Maurice?

MAURICE. [*Stops unwillingly*] What is it?

MME. CATHERINE. Don't do it! Don't do it!

MAURICE. What?

MME. CATHERINE. Don't do it!

MAURICE. Don't be scared. This lady is not my kind, but she interests me. Or hardly that even.

MME. CATHERINE. Don't trust yourself!

MAURICE. Yes, I do trust myself. Good-bye. [*Goes out.*

*Curtain.*

# ACT II

## FIRST SCENE

*The Auberge des Adrets: a café in sixteenth century style, with a suggestion of stage effect. Tables and easy-chairs are scattered in corners and nooks. The walls are decorated with armour and weapons. Along the ledge of the wainscoting stand glasses and jugs.*

MAURICE *and* HENRIETTE *are in evening dress and sit facing each other at a table on which stands a bottle of champagne and three filled glasses. The third glass is placed at that side of the table which is nearest the background, and there an easy-chair is kept ready for the still missing "third man."*

MAURICE. [*Puts his watch in front of himself on the table*] If he doesn't get here within the next five minutes, he isn't coming at all. And suppose in the meantime we drink with his ghost. [*Touches the third glass with the rim of his own.*

HENRIETTE. [*Doing the same*] Here's to you, Adolphe!

MAURICE. He won't come.

HENRIETTE. He will come.

MAURICE. He won't.

HENRIETTE. He will.

MAURICE. What an evening! What a wonderful day! I can hardly grasp that a new life has begun. Think only: the manager believes that I may count on no less than one hundred thousand francs. I'll spend twenty thousand on a villa outside the city. That leaves me eighty thousand. I won't be able to take it all in until to-morrow, for I am tired,

29

tired, tired. [*Sinks back into the chair*] Have you ever felt really happy?

HENRIETTE. Never. How does it feel?

MAURICE. I don't quite know how to put it. I cannot express it, but I seem chiefly to be thinking of the chagrin of my enemies. It isn't nice, but that's the way it is.

HENRIETTE. Is it happiness to be thinking of one's enemies?

MAURICE. Why, the victor has to count his killed and wounded enemies in order to gauge the extent of his victory.

HENRIETTE. Are you as bloodthirsty as all that?

MAURICE. Perhaps not. But when you have felt the pressure of other people's heels on your chest for years, it must be pleasant to shake off the enemy and draw a full breath at last.

HENRIETTE. Don't you find it strange that you are sitting here, alone with me, an insignificant girl practically unknown to you—and on an evening like this, when you ought to have a craving to show yourself like a triumphant hero to all the people, on the boulevards, in the big restaurants?

MAURICE. Of course, it's rather funny, but it feels good to be here, and your company is all I care for.

HENRIETTE. You don't look very hilarious.

MAURICE. No, I feel rather sad, and I should like to weep a little.

HENRIETTE. What is the meaning of that?

MAURICE. It is fortune conscious of its own nothingness and waiting for misfortune to appear.

HENRIETTE. Oh my, how sad! What is it you are missing anyhow?

MAURICE. I miss the only thing that gives value to life.

HENRIETTE. So you love her no longer then?

MAURICE. Not in the way I understand love. Do you

think she has read my play, or that she wants to see it?  Oh, she is so good, so self-sacrificing and considerate, but to go out with me for a night's fun she would regard as sinful. Once I treated her to champagne, you know, and instead of feeling happy over it, she picked up the wine list to see what it cost.  And when she read the price, she wept—wept because Marion was in need of new stockings.  It is beautiful, of course: it is touching, if you please.  But I can get no pleasure out of it.  And I do want a little pleasure before life runs out.  So far I have had nothing but privation, but now, now—life is beginning for me. [*The clock strikes twelve*] Now begins a new day, a new era!

HENRIETTE. Adolphe is not coming.

MAURICE. No, now he won't come.  And now it is too late to go back to the Crêmerie.

HENRIETTE. But they are waiting for you.

MAURICE. Let them wait.  They have made me promise to come, and I take back my promise.  Are you longing to go there?

HENRIETTE. On the contrary!

MAURICE. Will you keep me company then?

HENRIETTE. With pleasure, if you care to have me.

MAURICE. Otherwise I shouldn't be asking you.  It is strange, you know, that the victor's wreath seems worthless if you can't place it at the feet of some woman—that everything seems worthless when you have not a woman.

HENRIETTE. You don't need to be without a woman—you?

MAURICE. Well, that's the question.

HENRIETTE. Don't you know that a man is irresistible in his hour of success and fame?

MAURICE. No, I don't know, for I have had no experience of it.

HENRIETTE. You are a queer sort! At this moment, when you are the most envied man in Paris, you sit here and brood. Perhaps your conscience is troubling you because you have neglected that invitation to drink chicory coffee with the old lady over at the milk shop?

MAURICE. Yes, my conscience is troubling me on that score, and even here I am aware of their resentment, their hurt feelings, their well-grounded anger. My comrades in distress had the right to demand my presence this evening. The good Madame Catherine had a privileged claim on my success, from which a glimmer of hope was to spread over the poor fellows who have not yet succeeded. And I have robbed them of their faith in me. I can hear the vows they have been making: "Maurice will come, for he is a good fellow; he doesn't despise us, and he never fails to keep his word." Now I have made them forswear themselves.

> *While he is still speaking, somebody in the next room has begun to play the finale of Beethoven's Sonata in D-minor (Op. 31, No. 3). The allegretto is first played piano, then more forte, and at last passionately, violently, with complete abandon.*

MAURICE. Who can be playing at this time of the night?

HENRIETTE. Probably some nightbirds of the same kind as we. But listen! Your presentation of the case is not correct. Remember that Adolphe promised to meet us here. We waited for him, and he failed to keep his promise. So that you are not to blame——

MAURICE. You think so? While you are speaking, I believe you, but when you stop, my conscience begins again. What have you in that package?

HENRIETTE. Oh, it is only a laurel wreath that I meant to send up to the stage, but I had no chance to do so. Let me give it to you now—it is said to have a cooling effect on burning foreheads. [*She rises and crowns him with the wreath; then she kisses him on the forehead*] Hail to the victor!

MAURICE. Don't!

HENRIETTE. [*Kneeling*] Hail to the King!

MAURICE. [*Rising*] No, now you scare me.

HENRIETTE. You timid man! You of little faith who are afraid of fortune even! Who robbed you of your self-assurance and turned you into a dwarf?

MAURICE. A dwarf? Yes, you are right. I am not working up in the clouds, like a giant, with crashing and roaring, but I forge my weapons deep down in the silent heart of the mountain. You think that my modesty shrinks before the victor's wreath. On the contrary, I despise it: it is not enough for me. You think I am afraid of that ghost with its jealous green eyes which sits over there and keeps watch on my feelings—the strength of which you don't suspect. Away, ghost! [*He brushes the third, untouched glass off the table*] Away with you, you superfluous third person—you absent one who has lost your rights, if you ever had any. You stayed away from the field of battle because you knew yourself already beaten. As I crush this glass under my foot, so I will crush the image of yourself which you have reared in a temple no longer yours.

HENRIETTE. Good! That's the way! Well spoken, my hero!

MAURICE. Now I have sacrificed my best friend, my most faithful helper, on your altar, Astarte! Are you satisfied?

HENRIETTE. Astarte is a pretty name, and I'll keep it— I think you love me, Maurice.

MAURICE. Of course I do— Woman of evil omen, you who stir up man's courage with your scent of blood, whence do you come and where do you lead me? I loved you before I saw you, for I trembled when I heard them speak of you.

And when I saw you in the doorway, your soul poured itself into mine. And when you left, I could still feel your presence in my arms. I wanted to flee from you, but something held me back, and this evening we have been driven together as the prey is driven into the hunter's net. Whose is the fault? Your friend's, who pandered for us!

HENRIETTE. Fault or no fault: what does it matter, and what does it mean?— Adolphe has been at fault in not bringing us together before. He is guilty of having stolen from us two weeks of bliss, to which he had no right himself. I am jealous of him on your behalf. I hate him because he has cheated you out of your mistress. I should like to blot him from the host of the living, and his memory with him—wipe him out of the past even, make him unmade, unborn!

MAURICE. Well, we'll bury him beneath our own memories. We'll cover him with leaves and branches far out in the wild woods, and then we'll pile stone on top of the mound so that he will never look up again. [Raising his glass] Our fate is sealed. Woe unto us! What will come next?

HENRIETTE. Next comes the new era— What have you in that package?

MAURICE. I cannot remember.

HENRIETTE. [Opens the package and takes out a tie and a pair of gloves] That tie is a fright! It must have cost at least fifty centimes.

MAURICE. [Snatching the things away from her] Don't you touch them!

HENRIETTE. They are from her?

MAURICE. Yes, they are.

HENRIETTE. Give them to me.

MAURICE. No, she's better than we, better than everybody else.

HENRIETTE. I don't believe it. She is simply stupider and stingier. One who weeps because you order champagne——

MAURICE. When the child was without stockings. Yes, she is a good woman.

HENRIETTE. Philistine! You'll never be an artist. But I am an artist, and I'll make a bust of you with a shopkeeper's cap instead of the laurel wreath—Her name is Jeanne?

MAURICE. How do you know?

HENRIETTE. Why, that's the name of all housekeepers.

MAURICE. Henriette!

> HENRIETTE *takes the tie and the gloves and throws them into the fireplace.*

MAURICE. [*Weakly*] Astarte, now you demand the sacrifice of women. You shall have them, but if you ask for innocent children, too, then I'll send you packing.

HENRIETTE. Can you tell me what it is that binds you to me?

MAURICE. If I only knew, I should be able to tear myself away. But I believe it must be those qualities which you have and I lack. I believe that the evil within you draws me with the irresistible lure of novelty.

HENRIETTE. Have you ever committed a crime?

MAURICE. No real one. Have you?

HENRIETTE. Yes.

MAURICE. Well, how did you find it?

HENRIETTE. It was greater than to perform a good deed, for by that we are placed on equality with others; it was greater than to perform some act of heroism, for by that we are raised above others and rewarded. That crime placed me outside and beyond life, society, and my fellow-beings. Since then I am living only a partial life, a sort of dream life, and that's why reality never gets a hold on me.

MAURICE. What was it you did?

HENRIETTE. I won't tell, for then you would get scared again.

MAURICE. Can you never be found out?

HENRIETTE. Never. But that does not prevent me from seeing, frequently, the five stones at the Place de Roquette, where the scaffold used to stand; and for this reason I never dare to open a pack of cards, as I always turn up the five-spot of diamonds.

MAURICE. Was it that kind of a crime?

HENRIETTE. Yes, it was that kind.

MAURICE. Of course, it's horrible, but it is interesting. Have you no conscience?

HENRIETTE. None, but I should be grateful if you would talk of something else.

MAURICE. Suppose we talk of—love?

HENRIETTE. Of that you don't talk until it is over.

MAURICE. Have you been in love with Adolphe?

HENRIETTE. I don't know. The goodness of his nature drew me like some beautiful, all but vanished memory of childhood. Yet there was much about his person that offended my eye, so that I had to spend a long time retouching, altering, adding, subtracting, before I could make a presentable figure of him. When he talked, I could notice that he had learned from you, and the lesson was often badly digested and awkwardly applied. You can imagine then how miserable the copy must appear now, when I am permitted to study the original. That's why he was afraid of having us two meet; and when it did happen, he understood at once that his time was up.

MAURICE. Poor Adolphe!

HENRIETTE. I feel sorry for him, too, as I know he must be suffering beyond all bounds——

MAURICE. Sh! Somebody is coming.

HENRIETTE. I wonder if it could be he?

MAURICE. That would be unbearable.

HENRIETTE. No, it isn't he, but if it had been, how do you think the situation would have shaped itself?

MAURICE. At first he would have been a little sore at you because he had made a mistake in regard to the meeting-place—and tried to find us in several other cafés—but his soreness would have changed into pleasure at finding us—and seeing that we had not deceived him. And in the joy at having wronged us by his suspicions, he would love both of us. And so it would make him happy to notice that we had become such good friends. It had always been his dream —hm! he is making the speech now—his dream that the three of us should form a triumvirate that could set the world a great example of friendship asking for nothing— "Yes, I trust you, Maurice, partly because you are my friend, and partly because your feelings are tied up elsewhere."

HENRIETTE. Bravo! You must have been in a similar situation before, or you couldn't give such a lifelike picture of it. Do you know that Adolphe is just that kind of a third person who cannot enjoy his mistress without having his friend along?

MAURICE. That's why I had to be called in to entertain you— Hush! There is somebody outside— It must be he.

HENRIETTE. No, don't you know these are the hours when ghosts walk, and then you can see so many things, and hear them also. To keep awake at night, when you ought to be sleeping, has for me the same charm as a crime: it is to place oneself above and beyond the laws of nature.

MAURICE. But the punishment is fearful—I am shivering or quivering, with cold or with fear.

HENRIETTE. [*Wraps her opera cloak about him*] Put this on. It will make you warm.

MAURICE. That's nice. It is as if I were inside of your skin, as if my body had been melted up by lack of sleep and were being remoulded in your shape. I can feel the moulding process going on. But I am also growing a new soul, new thoughts, and here, where your bosom has left an impression, I can feel my own beginning to bulge.

*During this entire scene, the pianist in the next room has been practicing the Sonata in D-minor, sometimes pianissimo, sometimes wildly fortissimo; now and then he has kept silent for a little while, and at other times nothing has been heard but a part of the finale: bars 96 to 107.*

MAURICE. What a monster, to sit there all night practicing on the piano. It gives me a sick feeling. Do you know what I propose? Let us drive out to the Bois de Boulogne and take breakfast in the Pavilion, and see the sun rise over the lakes.

HENRIETTE. Bully!

MAURICE. But first of all I must arrange to have my mail and the morning papers sent out by messenger to the Pavilion. Tell me, Henriette: shall we invite Adolphe?

HENRIETTE. Oh, that's going too far! But why not? The ass can also be harnessed to the triumphal chariot. Let him come.                    [*They get up.*

MAURICE. [*Taking off the cloak*] Then I'll ring.

HENRIETTE. Wait a moment!

[*Throws herself into his arms.*

*Curtain.*

## SECOND SCENE

*A large, splendidly furnished restaurant room in the Bois de Boulogne. It is richly carpeted and full of mirrors, easy-chairs, and divans. There are glass doors in the back-ground, and beside them windows overlooking the lakes. In the foreground a table is spread, with flowers in the centre, bowls full of fruit, wine in decanters, oysters on platters, many different kinds of wine glasses, and two lighted candelabra. On the right there is a round table full of newspapers and telegrams.*

*MAURICE and HENRIETTE are sitting opposite each other at this small table.*

*The sun is just rising outside.*

MAURICE. There is no longer any doubt about it. The newspapers tell me it is so, and these telegrams congratulate me on my success. This is the beginning of a new life, and my fate is wedded to yours by this night, when you were the only one to share my hopes and my triumph. From your hand I received the laurel, and it seems to me as if every-thing had come from you.

HENRIETTE. What a wonderful night! Have we been dreaming, or is this something we have really lived through?

MAURICE. [*Rising*] And what a morning after such a night! I feel as if it were the world's first day that is now being illumined by the rising sun. Only this minute was the earth created and stripped of those white films that are now floating off into space. There lies the Garden of Eden in the rosy light of dawn, and here is the first human couple— Do you know, I am so happy I could cry at the thought that all mankind is not equally happy— Do you hear that distant murmur as of ocean waves beating against a rocky shore, as of winds sweeping through a forest? Do you know what it is? It is Paris whispering my name. Do you see the columns of smoke that rise skyward in thousands and tens of thousands? They are the fires burning on my altars, and if that be not so, then it must become so, for I will it. At this moment all the telegraph instruments of Europe are clicking out my name. The Oriental Express is carrying the newspapers to the Far East, toward the rising sun; and the ocean steamers are carrying them to the utmost West. The earth is mine, and for that reason it is beautiful. Now I should like to have wings for us two, so that we might rise from here and fly far, far away, before anybody can soil my happiness, before envy has a chance to wake me out of my dream—for it is probably a dream!

HENRIETTE. [*Holding out her hand to him*] Here you can feel that you are not dreaming.

MAURICE. It is not a dream, but it has been one. As a poor young man, you know, when I was walking in the woods down there, and looked up to this Pavilion, it looked to me like a fairy castle, and always my thoughts carried me up to this room, with the balcony outside and the heavy curtains, as to a place of supreme bliss. To be sitting here in company with a beloved woman and see the sun rise while the candles were still burning in the candelabra: that was the most audacious dream of my youth. Now it has come true, and now I have no more to ask of life— Do you want to die now, together with me?

HENRIETTE. No, you fool! Now I want to begin living.

MAURICE. [*Rising*] To live: that is to suffer! Now comes reality. I can hear his steps on the stairs. He is panting with alarm, and his heart is beating with dread of having lost what it holds most precious. Can you believe me if I

tell you that Adolphe is under this roof? Within a minute
he will be standing in the middle of this floor.

HENRIETTE. [*Alarmed*] It was a stupid trick to ask him
to come here, and I am already regretting it— Well, we
shall see anyhow if your forecast of the situation proves
correct.

MAURICE. Oh, it is easy to be mistaken about a person's
feelings.

*The* HEAD WAITER *enters with a card.*

MAURICE. Ask the gentleman to step in. [*To* HENRIETTE]
I am afraid we'll regret this.

HENRIETTE. Too late to think of that now— Hush!

ADOLPHE *enters, pale and hollow-eyed.*

MAURICE. [*Trying to speak unconcernedly*] There you are!
What became of you last night?

ADOLPHE. I looked for you at the Hôtel des Arrêts and
waited a whole hour.

MAURICE. So you went to the wrong place. We were
waiting several hours for you at the Auberge des Adrets, and
we are still waiting for you, as you see.

ADOLPHE. [*Relieved*] Thank heaven!

HENRIETTE. Good morning, Adolphe. You are always
expecting the worst and worrying yourself needlessly. I
suppose you imagined that we wanted to avoid your company. And though you see that we sent for you, you are
still thinking yourself superfluous.

ADOLPHE. Pardon me: I was wrong, but the night was
dreadful.

*They sit down. Embarrassed silence follows.*

HENRIETTE. [*To* ADOLPHE] Well, are you not going to
congratulate Maurice on his great success?

ADOLPHE. Oh, yes! Your success is the real thing, and
envy itself cannot deny it. Everything is giving way before

you, and even I have a sense of my own smallness in your presence.

MAURICE. Nonsense!— Henriette, are you not going to offer Adolphe a glass of wine?

ADOLPHE. Thank you, not for me—nothing at all!

HENRIETTE. [*To* ADOLPHE] What's the matter with you? Are you ill?

ADOLPHE. Not yet, but——

HENRIETTE. Your eyes——

ADOLPHE. What of them?

MAURICE. What happened at the Crêmerie last night? I suppose they are angry with me?

ADOLPHE. Nobody is angry with you, but your absence caused a depression which it hurt me to watch. But nobody was angry with you, believe me. Your friends understood, and they regarded your failure to come with sympathetic forbearance. Madame Catherine herself defended you and proposed your health. We all rejoiced in your success as if it had been our own.

HENRIETTE. Well, those are nice people! What good friends you have, Maurice.

MAURICE. Yes, better than I deserve.

ADOLPHE. Nobody has better friends than he deserves, and you are a man greatly blessed in his friends— Can't you feel how the air is softened to-day by all the kind thoughts and wishes that stream toward you from a thousand breasts?

MAURICE *rises in order to hide his emotion.*

ADOLPHE. From a thousand breasts that you have rid of the nightmare that had been crushing them during a lifetime. Humanity had been slandered—and you have exonerated it: that's why men feel grateful toward you. To-day they are once more holding their heads high and saying:

You see, we are a little better than our reputation after all. And that thought *makes* them better.

HENRIETTE *tries to hide her emotion.*

ADOLPHE. Am I in the way? Just let me warm myself a little in your sunshine, Maurice, and then I'll go.

MAURICE. Why should you go when you have only just arrived?

ADOLPHE. Why? Because I have seen what I need not have seen; because I know now that my hour is past. [*Pause*] That you sent for me, I take as an expression of thoughtfulness, a notice of what has happened, a frankness that hurts less than deceit. You hear that I think well of my fellow-beings, and this I have learned from you, Maurice. [*Pause*] But, my friend, a few moments ago I passed through the Church of St. Germain, and there I saw a woman and a child. I am not wishing that you had seen them, for what has happened cannot be altered, but if you gave a thought or a word to them before you set them adrift on the waters of the great city, then you could enjoy your happiness undisturbed. And now I bid you good-by.

HENRIETTE. Why must you go?

ADOLPHE. And you ask that? Do you want me to tell you?

HENRIETTE. No, I don't.

ADOLPHE. Good-by then!        [*Goes out.*

MAURICE. The Fall: and lo! "they knew that they were naked."

HENRIETTE. What a difference between this scene and the one we imagined! He is better than we.

MAURICE. It seems to me now as if all the rest were better than we.

HENRIETTE. Do you see that the sun has vanished behind clouds, and that the woods have lost their rose colour?

MAURICE. Yes, I see, and the blue lake has turned black. Let us flee to some place where the sky is always blue and the trees are always green.

HENRIETTE. Yes, let us—but without any farewells.

MAURICE. No, with farewells.

HENRIETTE. We were to fly. You spoke of wings—and your feet are of lead. I am not jealous, but if you go to say farewell and get two pairs of arms around your neck—then you can't tear yourself away.

MAURICE. Perhaps you are right, but only one pair of little arms is needed to hold me fast.

HENRIETTE. It is the child that holds you then, and not the woman?

MAURICE. It is the child.

HENRIETTE. The child! Another woman's child! And for the sake of it I am to suffer. Why must that child block the way where I want to pass, and must pass?

MAURICE. Yes, why? It would be better if it had never existed.

HENRIETTE. [Walks excitedly back and forth] Indeed! But now it does exist. Like a rock on the road, a rock set firmly in the ground, immovable, so that it upsets the carriage.

MAURICE. The triumphal chariot!— The ass is driven to death, but the rock remains. Curse it!            [Pause.

HENRIETTE. There is nothing to do.

MAURICE. Yes, we must get married, and then *our* child will make us forget the other one.

HENRIETTE. This will kill this!

MAURICE. Kill! What kind of word is that?

HENRIETTE. [Changing tone] Your child will kill our love.

MAURICE. No, girl, our love will kill whatever stands in its way, but it will not be killed.

HENRIETTE. [Opens a deck of cards lying on the mantlepiece]

Look at it! Five-spot of diamonds—the scaffold! Can it be possible that our fates are determined in advance? That our thoughts are guided as if through pipes to the spot for which they are bound, without chance for us to stop them? But I don't want it, I don't want it!— Do you realise that I must go to the scaffold if my crime should be discovered?

MAURICE. Tell me about your crime. Now is the time for it.

HENRIETTE. No, I should regret it afterward, and you would despise me—no, no, no!— Have you ever heard that a person could be hated to death? Well, my father incurred the hatred of my mother and my sisters, and he melted away like wax before a fire. Ugh! Let us talk of something else. And, above all, let us get away. The air is poisoned here. To-morrow your laurels will be withered, the triumph will be forgotten, and in a week another triumphant hero will hold the public attention. Away from here, to work for new victories! But first of all, Maurice, you must embrace your child and provide for its immediate future. You don't have to see the mother at all.

MAURICE. Thank you! Your good heart does you honour, and I love you doubly when you show the kindness you generally hide.

HENRIETTE. And then you go to the Crêmerie and say good-by to the old lady and your friends. Leave no unsettled business behind to make your mind heavy on our trip.

MAURICE. I'll clear up everything, and to-night we meet at the railroad station.

HENRIETTE. Agreed! And then: away from here—away toward the sea and the sun!


*Curtain.*

# ACT III

## FIRST SCENE

*In the Crêmerie. The gas is lit.* MME. CATHERINE *is seated at the counter,* ADOLPHE *at a table.*

MME. CATHERINE. Such is life, Monseiur Adolphe. But you young ones are always demanding too much, and then you come here and blubber over it afterward.

ADOLPHE. No, it isn't that. I reproach nobody, and I am as fond as ever of both of them. But there is one thing that makes me sick at heart. You see, I thought more of Maurice than of anybody else; so much that I wouldn't have grudged him anything that could give him pleasure—but now I have lost him, and it hurts me worse than the loss of her. I have lost both of them, and so my loneliness is made doubly painful. And then there is still something else which I have not yet been able to clear up.

MME. CATHERINE. Don't brood so much. Work and divert yourself. Now, for instance, do you ever go to church?

ADOLPHE. What should I do there?

MME. CATHERINE. Oh, there's so much to look at, and then there is the music. There is nothing commonplace about it, at least.

ADOLPHE. Perhaps not. But I don't belong to that fold, I guess, for it never stirs me to any devotion. And then, Madame Catherine, faith is a gift, they tell me, and I haven't got it yet.

MME. CATHERINE. Well, wait till you get it— But what is this I heard a while ago? Is it true that you have

46

sold a picture in London for a high price, and that you have
got a medal?

ADOLPHE. Yes, it's true.

MME. CATHERINE. Merciful heavens!—and not a word do
you say about it?

ADOLPHE. I am afraid of fortune, and besides it seems
almost worthless to me at this moment. I am afraid of it
as of a spectre: it brings disaster to speak of having seen it.

MME. CATHERINE. You're a queer fellow, and that's what
you have always been.

ADOLPHE. Not queer at all, but I have seen so much misfortune come in the wake of fortune, and I have seen how
adversity brings out true friends, while none but false ones
appear in the hour of success— You asked me if I ever
went to church, and I answered evasively. This morning I
stepped into the Church of St. Germain without really knowing why I did so. It seemed as if I were looking for somebody in there—somebody to whom I could silently offer my
gratitude. But I found nobody. Then I dropped a gold
coin in the poor-box. It was all I could get out of my church-
going, and that was rather commonplace, I should say.

MME. CATHERINE. It was always something; and then
it was fine to think of the poor after having heard good
news.

ADOLPHE. It was neither fine nor anything else: it was
something I did because I couldn't help myself. But something more occurred while I was in the church. I saw
Maurice's girl friend, Jeanne, and her child. Struck down,
crushed by his triumphal chariot, they seemed aware of the
full extent of their misfortune.

MME. CATHERINE. Well, children, I don't know in what
kind of shape you keep your consciences. But how a decent
fellow, a careful and considerate man like Monsieur Maurice,

can all of a sudden desert a woman and her child, that is something I cannot explain.

ADOLPHE. Nor can I explain it, and he doesn't seem to understand it himself. I met them this morning, and everything appeared quite natural to them, quite proper, as if they couldn't imagine anything else. It was as if they had been enjoying the satisfaction of a good deed or the fulfilment of a sacred duty. There are things, Madame Catherine, that we cannot explain, and for this reason it is not for us to judge. And besides, you saw how it happened. Maurice felt the danger in the air. I foresaw it and tried to prevent their meeting. Maurice wanted to run away from it, but nothing helped. Why, it was as if a plot had been laid by some invisible power, and as if they had been driven by guile into each other's arms. Of course, I am disqualified in this case, but I wouldn't hesitate to pronounce a verdict of "not guilty."

MME. CATHERINE. Well, now, to be able to forgive as you do, that's what I call religion.

ADOLPHE. Heavens, could it be that I am religious without knowing it.

MME. CATHERINE. But then, to *let* oneself be driven or tempted into evil, as Monsieur Maurice has done, means weakness or bad character. And if you feel your strength failing you, then you ask for help, and then you get it. But he was too conceited to do that— Who is this coming? The Abbé, I think.

ADOLPHE. What does he want here?

ABBÉ. [*Enters*] Good evening, madame. Good evening, Monsieur.

MME. CATHERINE. Can I be of any service?

ABBÉ. Has Monsieur Maurice, the author, been here to-day?

MME. CATHERINE. Not to-day. His play has just been put on, and that is probably keeping him busy.

ABBÉ. I have—sad news to bring him. Sad in several respects.

MME. CATHERINE. May I ask of what kind?

ABBÉ. Yes, it's no secret. The daughter he had with that girl, Jeanne, is dead.

MME. CATHERINE. Dead!

ADOLPHE. Marion dead!

ABBÉ. Yes, she died suddenly this morning without any previous illness.

MME. CATHERINE. O Lord, who can tell Thy ways!

ABBÉ. The mother's grief makes it necessary that Monsieur Maurice look after her, so we must try to find him. But first a question in confidence: do you know whether Monsieur Maurice was fond of the child, or was indifferent to it?

MME. CATHERINE. If he was fond of Marion? Why, all of us know how he loved her.

ADOLPHE. There's no doubt about that.

ABBÉ. I am glad to hear it, and it settles the matter so far as I am concerned.

MME. CATHERINE. Has there been any doubt about it?

ABBÉ. Yes, unfortunately. It has even been rumoured in the neighbourhood that he had abandoned the child and its mother in order to go away with a strange woman. In a few hours this rumour has grown into definite accusations, and at the same time the feeling against him has risen to such a point that his life is threatened and he is being called a murderer.

MME. CATHERINE. Good God, what is *this?* What does it mean?

ABBÉ. Now I'll tell you my opinion— I am convinced that the man is innocent on this score, and the mother feels as certain about it as I do. But appearances are against Monsieur Maurice, and I think he will find it rather hard to clear himself when the police come to question him.

ADOLPHE. Have the police got hold of the matter?

ABBÉ. Yes, the police have had to step in to protect him against all those ugly rumours and the rage of the people. Probably the Commissaire will be here soon.

MME. CATHERINE. [*To* ADOLPHE] There you see what happens when a man cannot tell the difference between good and evil, and when he trifles with vice. God will punish!

ADOLPHE. Then he is more merciless than man.

ABBÉ. What do you know about that?

ADOLPHE. Not very much, but I keep an eye on what happens——

ABBÉ. And you understand it also?

ADOLPHE. Not yet perhaps.

ABBÉ. Let us look more closely at the matter— Oh, here comes the Commissaire.

COMMISSAIRE. [*Enters*] Gentlemen—Madame Catherine— I have to trouble you for a moment with a few questions concerning Monsieur Maurice. As you have probably heard, he has become the object of a hideous rumour, which, by the by, I don't believe in.

MME. CATHERINE. None of us believes in it either.

COMMISSAIRE. That strengthens my own opinion, but for his own sake I must give him a chance to defend himself.

ABBÉ. That's right, and I guess he will find justice, although it may come hard.

COMMISSAIRE. Appearances are very much against him, but I have seen guiltless people reach the scaffold before their innocence was discovered. Let me tell you what there is against him. The little girl, Marion, being left alone by her

mother, was secretly visited by the father, who seems to
have made sure of the time when the child was to be found
alone. Fifteen minutes after his visit the mother returned
home and found the child dead. All this makes the position
of the accused man very unpleasant— The post-mortem
examination brought out no signs of violence or of poison,
but the physicians admit the existence of new poisons that
leave no traces behind them. To me all this is mere coincidence of the kind I frequently come across. But here's
something that looks worse. Last night Monsieur Maurice
was seen at the Auberge des Adrets in company with a strange
lady. According to the waiter, they were talking about
crimes. The Place de Roquette and the scaffold were both
mentioned. A queer topic of conversation for a pair of
lovers of good breeding and good social position! But even
this may be passed over, as we know by experience that
people who have been drinking and losing a lot of sleep seem
inclined to dig up all the worst that lies at the bottom of
their souls. Far more serious is the evidence given by the
head waiter as to their champagne breakfast in the Bois de
Boulogne this morning. He says that he heard them wish the
life out of a child. The man is said to have remarked that,
"It would be better if it had never existed." To which the
woman replied: "Indeed! But now it does exist." And as
they went on talking, these words occurred: "This will kill
this!" And the answer was: "Kill! What kind of word is
that?" And also: "The five-spot of diamonds, the scaffold,
the Place de Roquette." All this, you see, will be hard to
get out of, and so will the foreign journey planned for this
evening. These are serious matters.

ADOLPHE. He is lost!

MME. CATHERINE. That's a dreadful story. One doesn't
know what to believe.

ABBÉ. This is not the work of man. God have mercy on him!

ADOLPHE. He is in the net, and he will never get out of it.

MME. CATHERINE. He had no business to get in.

ADOLPHE. Do you begin to suspect him also, Madame Catherine?

MME. CATHERINE. Yes and no. I have got beyond having an opinion in this matter. Have you not seen angels turn into devils just as you turn your hand, and then become angels again?

COMMISSAIRE. It certainly does look queer. However, we'll have to wait and hear what explanations he can give. No one will be judged unheard. Good evening, gentlemen. Good evening, Madame Catherine. [*Goes out.*

ABBÉ. This is not the work of man.

ADOLPHE. No, it looks as if demons had been at work for the undoing of man.

ABBÉ. It is either a punishment for secret misdeeds, or it is a terrible test.

JEANNE. [*Enters, dressed in mourning*] Good evening. Pardon me for asking, but have you seen Monsieur Maurice?

MME. CATHERINE. No, madame, but I think he may be here any minute. You haven't met him then since——

JEANNE. Not since this morning.

MME. CATHERINE. Let me tell you that I share in your great sorrow.

JEANNE. Thank you, madame. [*To the* ABBÉ] So you are here, Father.

ABBÉ. Yes, my child. I thought I might be of some use to you. And it was fortunate, as it gave me a chance to speak to the Commissaire.

JEANNE. The Commissaire! He doesn't suspect Maurice also, does he?

ABBÉ. No, he doesn't, and none of us here do. But appearances are against him in a most appalling manner.

JEANNE. You mean on account of the talk the waiters overheard—it means nothing to me, who has heard such things before when Maurice had had a few drinks. Then it is his custom to speculate on crimes and their punishment. Besides it seems to have been the woman in his company who dropped the most dangerous remarks. I should like to have a look into that woman's eyes.

ADOLPHE. My dear Jeanne, no matter how much harm that woman may have done you, she did nothing with evil intention—in fact, she had no intention whatever, but just followed the promptings of her nature. I know her to be a good soul and one who can very well bear being looked straight in the eye.

JEANNE. Your judgment in this matter, Adolphe, has great value to me, and I believe what you say. It means that I cannot hold anybody but myself responsible for what has happened. It is my carelessness that is now being punished.                    [She begins to cry.

ABBÉ. Don't accuse yourself unjustly! I know you, and the serious spirit in which you have regarded your motherhood. That your assumption of this responsibility had not been sanctioned by religion and the civil law was not your fault. No, we are here facing something quite different.

ADOLPHE. What then?

ABBÉ. Who can tell?

HENRIETTE enters, dressed in travelling suit.

ADOLPHE. [Rises with an air of determination and goes to meet HENRIETTE] You here?

HENRIETTE. Yes, where is Maurice?

ADOLPHE. Do you know—or don't you?

HENRIETTE. I know everything. Excuse me, Madame

Catherine, but I was ready to start and absolutely had to step in here a moment. [*To* ADOLPHE] Who is that woman? —Oh!

HENRIETTE *and* JEANNE *stare at each other.*

EMILE *appears in the kitchen door.*

HENRIETTE. [*To* JEANNE] I ought to say something, but it matters very little, for anything I can say must sound like an insult or a mockery. But if I ask you simply to believe that I share your deep sorrow as much as anybody standing closer to you, then you must not turn away from me. You mustn't, for I deserve your pity if not your forbearance.

[*Holds out her hand.*

JEANNE. [*Looks hard at her*] I believe you now—and in the next moment I don't.          [*Takes* HENRIETTE'S *hand.*

HENRIETTE. [*Kisses* JEANNE'S *hand*] Thank you!

JEANNE. [*Drawing back her hand*] Oh, don't! I don't deserve it! I don't deserve it!

ABBÉ. Pardon me, but while we are gathered here and peace seems to prevail temporarily at least, won't you, Mademoiselle Henriette, shed some light into all the uncertainty and darkness surrounding the main point of accusation? I ask you, as a friend among friends, to tell us what you meant with all that talk about killing, and crime, and the Place de Roquette. That your words had no connection with the death of the child, we have reason to believe, but it would give us added assurance to hear what you were really talking about. Won't you tell us?

HENRIETTE. [*After a pause*] That I cannot tell! No, I cannot!

ADOLPHE. Henriette, do tell! Give us the word that will relieve us all.

HENRIETTE. I cannot! Don't ask me!

ABBÉ. This is not the work of man!

HENRIETTE. Oh, that this moment had to come! And in this manner! [*To* JEANNE] Madame, I swear that I am not guilty of your child's death. Is that enough?

JEANNE. Enough for us, but not for Justice.

HENRIETTE. Justice! If you knew how true your words are!

ABBÉ. [*To* HENRIETTE] And if you knew what you were saying just now!

HENRIETTE. Do you know that better than I?

ABBÉ. Yes, I do.

HENRIETTE *looks fixedly at the* ABBÉ.

ABBÉ. Have no fear, for even if I guess your secret, it will not be exposed. Besides, I have nothing to do with human justice, but a great deal with divine mercy.

MAURICE. [*Enters hastily, dressed for travelling. He doesn't look at the others, who are standing in the background, but goes straight up to the counter, where* MME. CATHERINE *is sitting.*] You are not angry at me, Madame Catherine, because I didn't show up. I have come now to apologise to you before I start for the South at eight o'clock this evening.

MME. CATHERINE *is too startled to say a word.*

MAURICE. Then you are angry at me? [*Looks around*] What does all this mean? Is it a dream, or what is it? Of course, I can see that it is all real, but it looks like a wax cabinet— There is Jeanne, looking like a statue and dressed in black— And Henriette looking like a corpse— What does it mean?

*All remain silent.*

MAURICE. Nobody answers. It must mean something dreadful. [*Silence*] But speak, please! Adolphe, you are my friend, what is it? [*Pointing to* EMILE] And there is a detective!

ADOLPHE. [*Comes forward*] You don't know then?

MAURICE. Nothing at all. But I must know!

ADOLPHE. Well, then—Marion is dead.

MAURICE. Marion—dead?

ADOLPHE. Yes, she died this morning.

MAURICE. [*To* JEANNE] So that's why you are in mourning. Jeanne, Jeanne, who has done this to us?

JEANNE. He who holds life and death in his hand.

MAURICE. But I saw her looking well and happy this morning. How did it happen? Who did it? Somebody must have done it?          [*His eyes seek* HENRIETTE.

ADOLPHE. Don't look for the guilty one here, for there is none to be found. Unfortunately the police have turned their suspicion in a direction where none ought to exist.

MAURICE. What direction is that?

ADOLPHE. Well—you may as well know that your reckless talk last night and this morning has placed you in a light that is anything but favourable.

MAURICE. So they were listening to us. Let me see, what were we saying—I remember!— Then I am lost!

ADOLPHE. But if you explain your thoughtless words we will believe you.

MAURICE. I cannot! And I will not! I shall be sent to prison, but it doesn't matter. Marion is dead! Dead! And I have killed her!

*General consternation.*

ADOLPHE. Think of what you are saying! Weigh your words! Do you realise what you said just now?

MAURICE. What did I say?

ADOLPHE. You said that you had killed Marion.

MAURICE. Is there a human being here who could believe me a murderer, and who could hold me capable of taking my own child's life? You who know me, Madame Catherine, tell me: do you believe, can you believe——

MME. CATHERINE. I don't know any longer what to believe. What the heart thinketh the tongue speaketh. And your tongue has spoken evil words.

MAURICE. She doesn't believe me!

ADOLPHE. But explain your words, man! Explain what you meant by saying that "your love would kill everything that stood in its way."

MAURICE. So they know that too— Are you willing to explain it, Henriette?

HENRIETTE. No, I cannot do that.

ABBÉ. There is something wrong behind all this and you have lost our sympathy, my friend. A while ago I could have sworn that you were innocent, and I wouldn't do that now.

MAURICE. [*To* JEANNE] What you have to say means more to me than anything else.

JEANNE. [*Coldly*] Answer a question first: who was it you cursed during that orgie out there?

MAURICE. Have I done that too? Maybe. Yes, I am guilty, and yet I am guiltless. Let me go away from here, for I am ashamed of myself, and I have done more wrong than I can forgive myself.

HENRIETTE. [*To* ADOLPHE] Go with him and see that he doesn't do himself any harm.

ADOLPHE. Shall I——?

HENRIETTE. Who else?

ADOLPHE. [*Without bitterness*] You are nearest to it— Sh! A carriage is stopping outside.

MME. CATHERINE. It's the Commissaire. Well, much as I have seen of life, I could never have believed that success and fame were such short-lived things.

MAURICE. [*To* HENRIETTE] From the triumphal chariot to the patrol wagon!

JEANNE. [*Simply*] And the ass—who was that?

ADOLPHE. Oh, that must have been me.

COMMISSAIRE. [*Enters with a paper in his hand*] A summons to Police Headquarters—to-night, at once—for Monsieur Maurice Gérard—and for Mademoiselle Henriette Mauclerc —both here?

MAURICE *and* HENRIETTE. Yes.

MAURICE. Is this an arrest?

COMMISSAIRE. Not yet.   Only a summons.

MAURICE. And then?

COMMISSAIRE. We don't know yet.

MAURICE *and* HENRIETTE *go toward the door.*

MAURICE. Good-bye to all!

*Everybody shows emotion.   The* COMMISSAIRE, MAURICE, *and* HENRIETTE *go out.*

EMILE. [*Enters and goes up to* JEANNE] Now I'll take you home, sister.

JEANNE. And what do you think of all this?

EMILE. The man is innocent.

ABBÉ. But as I see it, it is, and must always be, something despicable to break one's promise, and it becomes unpardonable when a woman and her child are involved.

EMILE. Well, I should rather feel that way, too, now when it concerns my own sister, but unfortunately I am prevented from throwing the first stone because I have done the same thing myself.

ABBÉ. Although I am free from blame in that respect, I am not throwing any stones either, but the act condemns itself and is punished by its consequences.

JEANNE. Pray for him!   For both of them!

ABBÉ. No, I'll do nothing of the kind, for it is an impertinence to want to change the counsels of the Lord.   And what has happened here is, indeed, not the work of man.

*Curtain.*

## SECOND SCENE

*The Auberge des Adrets.* ADOLPHE *and* HENRIETTE *are seated at the same table where* MAURICE *and* HENRIETTE *were sitting in the second act. A cup of coffee stands in front of* ADOLPHE. HENRIETTE *has ordered nothing.*

ADOLPHE. You believe then that he will come here?

HENRIETTE. I am sure. He was released this noon for lack of evidence, but he didn't want to show himself in the streets before it was dark.

ADOLPHE. Poor fellow! Oh, I tell you, life seems horrible to me since yesterday.

HENRIETTE. And what about me? I am afraid to live, dare hardly breathe, dare hardly think even, since I know that somebody is spying not only on my words but on my thoughts.

ADOLPHE. So it was here you sat that night when I couldn't find you?

HENRIETTE. Yes, but don't talk of it. I could die from shame when I think of it. Adolphe, you are made of a different, a better, stuff than he or I——

ADOLPHE. Sh, sh, sh!

HENRIETTE. Yes, indeed! And what was it that made me stay here? I was lazy; I was tired; his success intoxicated me and bewitched me—I cannot explain it. But if you had come, it would never have happened. And to-day you are great, and he is small—less than the least of all. Yesterday he had one hundred thousand francs. To-day he has nothing, because his play has been withdrawn. And public opinion will never excuse him, for his lack of faith will be judged as harshly as if he were the murderer, and those that see farthest hold that the child died from sorrow, so that he was responsible for it anyhow.

ADOLPHE. You know what my thoughts are in this matter, Henriette, but I should like to know that both of you are spotless. Won't you tell me what those dreadful words of yours meant? It cannot be a chance that your talk in a festive moment like that dealt so largely with killing and the scaffold.

HENRIETTE. It was no chance. It was something that had to be said, something I cannot tell you—probably because I have no right to appear spotless in your eyes, seeing that I am not spotless.

ADOLPHE. All this is beyond me.

HENRIETTE. Let us talk of something else— Do you believe there are many unpunished criminals at large among us, some of whom may even be our intimate friends?

ADOLPHE. [*Nervously*] Why? What do you mean?

HENRIETTE. Don't you believe that every human being at some time or another has been guilty of some kind of act which would fall under the law if it were discovered?

ADOLPHE. Yes, I believe that is true, but no evil act escapes being punished by one's own conscience at least. [*Rises and unbuttons his coat*] And—nobody is really good who has not erred. [*Breathing heavily*] For in order to know how to forgive, one must have been in need of forgiveness— I had a friend whom we used to regard as a model man. He never spoke a hard word to anybody; he forgave everything and everybody; and he suffered insults with a strange satisfaction that we couldn't explain. At last, late in life, he gave me his secret in a single word: I am a penitent!

[*He sits down again.*

HENRIETTE *remains silent, looking at him with surprise.*

ADOLPHE. [*As if speaking to himself*] There are crimes not

mentioned in the Criminal Code, and these are the worse ones, for they have to be punished by ourselves, and no judge could be more severe than we are against our own selves.

HENRIETTE. [*After a pause*] Well, that friend of yours, did he find peace?

ADOLPHE. After endless self-torture he reached a certain degree of composure, but life had never any real pleasures to offer him. He never dared to accept any kind of distinction; he never dared to feel himself entitled to a kind word or even well-earned praise: in a word, he could never quite forgive himself.

HENRIETTE. Never? What had he done then?

ADOLPHE. He had wished the life out of his father. And when his father suddenly died, the son imagined himself to have killed him. Those imaginations were regarded as signs of some mental disease, and he was sent to an asylum. From this he was discharged after a time as wholly recovered—as they put it. But the sense of guilt remained with him, and so he continued to punish himself for his evil thoughts.

HENRIETTE. Are you sure the evil will cannot kill?

ADOLPHE. You mean in some mystic way?

HENRIETTE. As you please. Let it go at mystic. In my own family—I am sure that my mother and my sisters killed my father with their hatred. You see, he had the awful idea that he must oppose all our tastes and inclinations. Wherever he discovered a natural gift, he tried to root it out. In that way he aroused a resistance that accumulated until it became like an electrical battery charged with hatred. At last it grew so powerful that he languished away, became depolarised, lost his will-power, and, in the end, came to wish himself dead.

ADOLPHE. And your conscience never troubled you?

HENRIETTE. No, and furthermore, I don't know what conscience is.

ADOLPHE. You don't? Well, then you'll soon learn. [*Pause*] How do you believe Maurice will look when he gets here? What do you think he will say?

HENRIETTE. Yesterday morning, you know, he and I tried to make the same kind of guess about you while we were waiting for you.

ADOLPHE. Well?

HENRIETTE. We guessed entirely wrong.

ADOLPHE. Can you tell me why you sent for me?

HENRIETTE. Malice, arrogance, outright cruelty!

ADOLPHE. How strange it is that you can admit your faults and yet not repent of them.

HENRIETTE. It must be because I don't feel quite responsible for them. They are like the dirt left behind by things handled during the day and washed off at night. But tell me one thing: do you really think so highly of humanity as you profess to do?

ADOLPHE. Yes, we are a little better than our reputation— and a little worse.

HENRIETTE. That is not a straightforward answer.

ADOLPHE. No, it isn't. But are you willing to answer me frankly when I ask you: do you still love Maurice?

HENRIETTE. I cannot tell until I see him. But at this moment I feel no longing for him, and it seems as if I could very well live without him.

ADOLPHE. It's likely you could, but I fear you have become chained to his fate—Sh! Here he comes.

HENRIETTE. How everything repeats itself. The situation is the same, the very words are the same, as when we were expecting you yesterday.

MAURICE. [*Enters, pale as death, hollow-eyed, unshaven*] Here I am, my dear friends, if this be me. For that last night in a cell changed me into a new sort of being.

[*Notices* HENRIETTE *and* ADOLPHE.

ADOLPHE. Sit down and pull yourself together, and then we can talk things over.

MAURICE. [*To* HENRIETTE] Perhaps I am in the way?

ADOLPHE. Now, don't get bitter.

MAURICE. I have grown bad in these twenty-four hours, and suspicious also, so I guess I'll soon be left to myself. And who wants to keep company with a murderer?

HENRIETTE. But you have been cleared of the charge.

MAURICE. [*Picks up a newspaper*] By the police, yes, but not by public opinion. Here you see the murderer Maurice Gérard, once a playwright, and his mistress, Henriette Mauclerc——

HENRIETTE. O my mother and my sisters—my mother! Jesus have mercy!

MAURICE. And can you see that I actually look like a murderer? And then it is suggested that my play was stolen. So there isn't a vestige left of the victorious hero from yesterday. In place of my own, the name of Octave, my enemy, appears on the bill-boards, and he is going to collect my one hundred thousand francs. O Solon, Solon! Such is fortune, and such is fame! You are fortunate, Adolphe, because you have not yet succeeded.

HENRIETTE. So you don't know that Adolphe has made a great success in London and carried off the first prize?

MAURICE. [*Darkly*] No, I didn't know that. Is it true, Adolphe?

ADOLPHE. It is true, but I have returned the prize.

HENRIETTE. [*With emphasis*] That I didn't know! So you

are also prevented from accepting any distinctions—like your friend?

ADOLPHE. My friend? [*Embarrassed*] Oh, yes, yes!

MAURICE. Your success gives me pleasure, but it puts us still farther apart.

ADOLPHE. That's what I expected, and I suppose I'll be as lonely with my success as you with your adversity. Think of it—that people feel hurt by your fortune! Oh, it's ghastly to be alive!

MAURICE. You say that! What am I then to say? It is as if my eyes had been covered with a black veil, and as if the colour and shape of all life had been changed by it. This room looks like the room I saw yesterday, and yet it is quite different. I recognise both of you, of course, but your faces are new to me. I sit here and search for words because I don't know what to say to you. I ought to defend myself, but I cannot. And I almost miss the cell, for it protected me, at least, against the curious glances that pass right through me. The murderer Maurice and his mistress! You don't love me any longer, Henriette, and no more do I care for you. To-day you are ugly, clumsy, insipid, repulsive.

> *Two men in civilian clothes have quietly seated themselves at a table in the background.*

ADOLPHE. Wait a little and get your thoughts together. That you have been discharged and cleared of all suspicion must appear in some of the evening papers. And that puts an end to the whole matter. Your play will be put on again, and if it comes to the worst, you can write a new one. Leave Paris for a year and let everything become forgotten. You who have exonerated mankind will be exonerated yourself.

MAURICE. Ha-ha! Mankind! Ha-ha!

ADOLPHE. You have ceased to believe in goodness?

MAURICE. Yes, if I ever did believe in it. Perhaps it was

only a mood, a manner of looking at things, a way of being polite to the wild beasts.   When I, who was held among the best, can be so rotten to the core, what must then be the wretchedness of the rest?

ADOLPHE.  Now I'll go out and get all the evening papers, and then we'll undoubtedly have reason to look at things in a different way.

MAURICE.  [*Turning toward the background*]  Two detectives! —It means that I am released under surveillance, so that I can give myself away by careless talking.

ADOLPHE.  Those are not detectives.   That's only your imagination.   I recognise both of them.

[*Goes toward the door.*

MAURICE.  Don't leave us alone, Adolphe.   I fear that Henriette and I may come to open explanations.

ADOLPHE.  Oh, be sensible, Maurice, and think of your future.   Try to keep him quiet, Henriette.   I'll be back in a moment.                                                    [*Goes out.*

HENRIETTE.  Well, Maurice, what do you think now of our guilt or guiltlessness?

MAURICE.  I have killed nobody.   All I did was to talk a lot of nonsense while I was drunk.   But it is your crime that comes back, and that crime you have grafted on to me.

HENRIETTE.  Oh, that's the tone you talk in now!—Was it not you who cursed your own child, and wished the life out of it, and wanted to go away without saying good-bye to any-body?   And was it not I who made you visit Marion and show yourself to Madame Catherine?

MAURICE.  Yes, you are right.   Forgive me!   You proved yourself more human than I, and the guilt is wholly my own. Forgive me!   But all the same I am without guilt.   Who has tied this net from which I can never free myself?   Guilty and guiltless: guiltless and yet guilty!   Oh, it is driving me mad— Look, now they sit over there and listen to us— And no waiter comes to take our order. I'll go out and order a cup of tea. Do you want anything?

HENRIETTE. Nothing.

MAURICE *goes out.*

FIRST DETECTIVE. [*Goes up to* HENRIETTE] Let me look at your papers.

HENRIETTE. How dare you speak to me?

DETECTIVE. Dare? I'll show you!

HENRIETTE. What do you mean?

DETECTIVE. It's my job to keep an eye on street-walkers. Yesterday you came here with one man, and to-day with another. That's as good as walking the streets. And un-escorted ladies don't get anything here. So you'd better get out and come along with me.

HENRIETTE. My escort will be back in a moment.

DETECTIVE. Yes, and a pretty kind of escort you've got— the kind that doesn't help a girl a bit!

HENRIETTE. O God! My mother, my sisters!— I am of good family, I tell you.

DETECTIVE. Yes, first-rate family, I am sure. But you are too well known through the papers. Come along!

HENRIETTE. Where? What do you mean?

DETECTIVE. Oh, to the Bureau, of course. There you'll get a nice little card and a license that brings you free medical care.

HENRIETTE. O Lord Jesus, you don't mean it!

DETECTIVE. [*Grabbing* HENRIETTE *by the arm*] Don't I mean it?

HENRIETTE. [*Falling on her knees*] Save me, Maurice! Help!

DETECTIVE. Shut up, you fool!

MAURICE *enters, followed by* WAITER.

WAITER. Gentlemen of that kind are not served here. You just pay and get out! And take the girl along!

MAURICE. [*Crushed, searches his pocket-book for money*] Henriette, pay for me, and let us get away from this place. I haven't a sou left.

WAITER. So the lady has to put up for her Alphonse! Alphonse! Do you know what that is?

HENRIETTE. [*Looking through her pocket-book*] Oh, merciful heavens! I have no money either!—Why doesn't Adolphe come back?

DETECTIVE. Well, did you ever see such rotters! Get out of here, and put up something as security. That kind of ladies generally have their fingers full of rings.

MAURICE. Can it be possible that we have sunk so low?

HENRIETTE. [*Takes off a ring and hands it to the* WAITER] The Abbé was right: this is not the work of man.

MAURICE. No, it's the devil's!— But if we leave before Adolphe returns, he will think that we have deceived him and run away.

HENRIETTE. That would be in keeping with the rest— But we'll go into the river now, won't we?

MAURICE. [*Takes* HENRIETTE *by the hand as they walk out together*] Into the river—yes!

*Curtain.*

# ACT IV

## FIRST SCENE

*In the Luxembourg Gardens, at the group of Adam and Eve.
The wind is shaking the trees and stirring up dead leaves,
straws, and pieces of paper from the ground.*

MAURICE *and* HENRIETTE *are seated on a bench.*

HENRIETTE. So you don't want to die?

MAURICE. No, I am afraid. I imagine that I am going
to be very cold down there in the grave, with only a sheet to
cover me and a few shavings to lie on. And besides that, it
seems to me as if there were still some task waiting for me,
but I cannot make out what it is.

HENRIETTE. But I can guess what it is.

MAURICE. Tell me.

HENRIETTE. It is revenge. You, like me, must have sus-
pected Jeanne and Emile of sending the detectives after me
yesterday. Such a revenge on a rival none but a woman
could devise.

MAURICE. Exactly what I was thinking. But let me tell
you that my suspicions go even further. It seems as if my
sufferings during these last few days had sharpened my wits.
Can you explain, for instance, why the waiter from the
Auberge des Adrets and the head waiter from the Pavilion
were not called to testify at the hearing?

HENRIETTE. I never thought of it before. But now I
know why. They had nothing to tell, because they had not
been listening.

MAURICE. But how could the Commissaire then know what we had been saying?

HENRIETTE. He didn't know, but he figured it out. He was guessing, and he guessed right. Perhaps he had had to deal with some similar case before.

MAURICE. Or else he concluded from our looks what we had been saying. There are those who can read other people's thoughts— Adolphe being the dupe, it seemed quite natural that we should have called him an ass. It's the rule, I understand, although it's varied at times by the use of "idiot" instead. But ass was nearer at hand in this case, as we had been talking of carriages and triumphal chariots. It is quite simple to figure out a fourth fact, when you have three known ones to start from.

HENRIETTE. Just think that we have let ourselves be taken in so completely.

MAURICE. That's the result of thinking too well of one's fellow beings. This is all you get out of it. But do you know, I suspect somebody else back of the Commissaire, who, by-the-bye, must be a full-fledged scoundrel.

HENRIETTE. You mean the Abbé, who was taking the part of a private detective.

MAURICE. That's what I mean. That man has to receive all kinds of confessions. And note you: Adolphe himself told us he had been at the Church of St. Germain that morning. What was he doing there? He was blabbing, of course, and bewailing his fate. And then the priest put the questions together for the Commissaire.

HENRIETTE. Tell me something: do you trust Adolphe?

MAURICE. I trust no human being any longer.

HENRIETTE. Not even Adolphe?

MAURICE. Him least of all. How could I trust an enemy —a man from whom I have taken away his mistress?

HENRIETTE. Well, as you were the first one to speak of this, I'll give you some data about our friend. You heard he had returned that medal from London. Do you know his reason for doing so?

MAURICE. No.

HENRIETTE. He thinks himself unworthy of it, and he has taken a penitential vow never to receive any kind of distinction.

MAURICE. Can that be possible? But what has he done?

HENRIETTE. He has committed a crime of the kind that is not punishable under the law. That's what he gave me to understand indirectly.

MAURICE. He, too! He, the best one of all, the model man, who never speaks a hard word of anybody and who forgives everything.

HENRIETTE. Well, there you can see that we are no worse than others. And yet we are being hounded day and night as if devils were after us.

MAURICE. He, also! Then mankind has not been slandered— But if he has been capable of *one* crime, then you may expect anything of him. Perhaps it was he who sent the police after you yesterday. Coming to think of it now, it was he who sneaked away from us when he saw that we were in the papers, and he lied when he insisted that those fellows were not detectives. But, of course, you may expect anything from a deceived lover.

HENRIETTE. Could he be as mean as that? No, it is impossible, impossible!

MAURICE. Why so? If he is a scoundrel?— What were you two talking of yesterday, before I came?

HENRIETTE. He had nothing but good to say of you.

MAURICE. That's a lie!

HENRIETTE. [*Controlling herself and changing her tone*]

Listen. There is one person on whom you have cast no suspicion whatever—for what reason, I don't know. Have you thought of Madame Catherine's wavering attitude in this matter? Didn't she say finally that she believed you capable of anything?

MAURICE. Yes, she did, and that shows what kind of person she is. To think evil of other people without reason, you must be a villain yourself.

HENRIETTE *looks hard at him. Pause.*

HENRIETTE. To think evil of others, you must be a villain yourself.

MAURICE. What do you mean?

HENRIETTE. What I said.

MAURICE. Do you mean that I——?

HENRIETTE. Yes, that's what I mean now! Look here! Did you meet anybody but Marion when you called there yesterday morning?

MAURICE. Why do you ask?

HENRIETTE. Guess!

MAURICE. Well, as you seem to know—I met Jeanne, too.

HENRIETTE. Why did you lie to me?

MAURICE. I wanted to spare you.

HENRIETTE. And now you want me to believe in one who has been lying to me? No, my boy, now I believe you guilty of that murder.

MAURICE. Wait a moment! We have now reached the place for which my thoughts have been heading all the time, though I resisted as long as possible. It's queer that what lies next to one is seen last of all, and what one doesn't *want* to believe cannot be believed— Tell me something: where did you go yesterday morning, after we parted in the Bois?

HENRIETTE. [*Alarmed*] Why?

MAURICE. You went either to Adolphe—which you couldn't do, as he was attending a lesson—or you went to—Marion!

HENRIETTE. Now I am convinced that you are the murderer.

MAURICE. And I, that you are the murderess! You alone had an interest in getting the child out of the way—to get rid of the rock on the road, as you so aptly put it.

HENRIETTE. It was you who said that.

MAURICE. And the one who had an interest in it must have committed the crime.

HENRIETTE. Now, Maurice, we have been running around and around in this tread-mill, scourging each other. Let us quit before we get to the point of sheer madness.

MAURICE. You have reached that point already.

HENRIETTE. Don't you think it's time for us to part, before we drive each other insane?

MAURICE. Yes, I think so.

HENRIETTE. [*Rising*] Good-bye then!

> *Two men in civilian clothes become visible in the back-*
> *ground.*

HENRIETTE. [*Turns and comes back to* MAURICE] There they are again!

MAURICE. The dark angels that want to drive us out of the garden.

HENRIETTE. And force us back upon each other as if we were chained together.

MAURICE. Or as if we were condemned to lifelong marriage. Are we really to marry? To settle down in the same place? To be able to close the door behind us and perhaps get peace at last?

HENRIETTE. And shut ourselves up in order to torture each other to death; get behind locks and bolts, with a ghost for marriage portion; you torturing me with the memory of Adolphe, and I getting back at you with Jeanne—and Marion.

MAURICE. Never mention the name of Marion again! Don't you know that she was to be buried to-day—at this very moment perhaps?

HENRIETTE. And you are not there? What does that mean?

MAURICE. It means that both Jeanne and the police have warned me against the rage of the people.

HENRIETTE. A coward, too?

MAURICE. All the vices! How could you ever have cared for me?

HENRIETTE. Because two days ago you were another person, well worthy of being loved——

MAURICE. And now sunk to such a depth!

HENRIETTE. It isn't that. But you are beginning to flaunt bad qualities which are not your own.

MAURICE. But yours?

HENRIETTE. Perhaps, for when you appear a little worse I feel myself at once a little better.

MAURICE. It's like passing on a disease to save one's self-respect.

HENRIETTE. And how vulgar you have become, too!

MAURICE. Yes, I notice it myself, and I hardly recognise myself since that night in the cell. They put in one person and let out another through that gate which separates us from the rest of society. And now I feel myself the enemy of all mankind: I should like to set fire to the earth and dry up the oceans, for nothing less than a universal conflagration can wipe out my dishonour.

HENRIETTE. I had a letter from my mother to-day. She is the widow of a major in the army, well educated, with old-fashioned ideas of honour and that kind of thing. Do you want to read the letter? No, you don't!— Do you know that I am an outcast? My respectable acquaintances will have nothing to do with me, and if I show myself on the streets alone the police will take me. Do you realise now that we have to get married?

MAURICE. We despise each other, and yet we have to marry: that is hell pure and simple! But, Henriette, before we unite our destinies you must tell me your secret, so that we may be on more equal terms.

HENRIETTE. All right, I'll tell you. I had a friend who got into trouble—you understand. I wanted to help her, as her whole future was at stake—and she died!

MAURICE. That was reckless, but one might almost call it noble, too.

HENRIETTE. You say so now, but the next time you lose your temper you will accuse me of it.

MAURICE. No, I won't. But I cannot deny that it has shaken my faith in you and that it makes me afraid of you. Tell me, is her lover still alive, and does he know to what extent you were responsible?

HENRIETTE. He was as guilty as I.

MAURICE. And if his conscience should begin to trouble him—such things do happen—and if he should feel inclined to confess: then you would be lost.

HENRIETTE. I know it, and it is this constant dread which has made me rush from one dissipation to another—so that I should never have time to wake up to full consciousness.

MAURICE. And now you want me to take my marriage portion out of your dread. That's asking a little too much.

HENRIETTE. But when I shared the shame of Maurice the murderer——

MAURICE. Oh, let's come to an end with it!

HENRIETTE. No, the end is not yet, and I'll not let go my

hold until I have put you where you belong. For you can't go around thinking yourself better than I am.

MAURICE. So you want to fight me then? All right, as you please!

HENRIETTE. A fight on life and death!

*The rolling of drums is heard in the distance.*

MAURICE. The garden is to be closed. "Cursed is the ground for thy sake; thorns and thistles shall it bring forth to thee."

HENRIETTE. "And the Lord God said unto the woman——"

A GUARD. [*In uniform, speaking very politely*] Sorry, but the garden has to be closed.

*Curtain.*

## SECOND SCENE

*The Crêmerie.* MME. CATHERINE *is sitting at the counter making entries into an account book.* ADOLPHE *and* HENRIETTE *are seated at a table.*

ADOLPHE. [*Calmly and kindly*] But if I give you my final assurance that I didn't run away, but that, on the contrary, I thought you had played me false, this ought to convince you.

HENRIETTE. But why did you fool us by saying that those fellows were not policemen?

ADOLPHE. I didn't think myself that they were, and then I wanted to reassure you.

HENRIETTE. When you say it, I believe you. But then you must also believe me, if I reveal my innermost thoughts to you.

ADOLPHE. Go on.

HENRIETTE. But you mustn't come back with your usual talk of fancies and delusions.

ADOLPHE. You seem to have reason to fear that I may.

HENRIETTE. I fear nothing, but I know you and your scepticism— Well, and then you mustn't tell this to anybody—promise me!

ADOLPHE. I promise.

HENRIETTE. Now think of it, although I must say it's something terrible: I have partial evidence that Maurice is guilty, or at least, I have reasonable suspicions——

ADOLPHE. You don't mean it!

HENRIETTE. Listen, and judge for yourself. When Maurice left me in the Bois, he said he was going to see Marion alone, as the mother was out. And now I have discovered afterward that he did meet the mother. So that he has been lying to me.

ADOLPHE. That's possible, and his motive for doing so may have been the best, but how can anybody conclude from it that he is guilty of a murder?

HENRIETTE. Can't you see that?— Don't you understand?

ADOLPHE. Not at all.

HENRIETTE. Because you don't want to!— Then there is nothing left for me but to report him, and we'll see whether he can prove an alibi.

ADOLPHE. Henriette, let me tell you the grim truth. You, like he, have reached the border line of—insanity. The demons of distrust have got hold of you, and each of you is using his own sense of partial guilt to wound the other with. Let me see if I can make a straight guess: he has also come to suspect you of killing his child?

HENRIETTE. Yes, he's mad enough to do so.

ADOLPHE. You call his suspicions mad, but not your own.

HENRIETTE. You have first to prove the contrary, or that I suspect him unjustly.

ADOLPHE. Yes, that's easy. A new autopsy has proved that Marion died of a well-known disease, the queer name of which I cannot recall just now.

HENRIETTE. Is it true?

ADOLPHE. The official report is printed in to-day's paper.

HENRIETTE. I don't take any stock in it. They can make up that kind of thing.

ADOLPHE. Beware, Henriette—or you may, without knowing it, pass across that border line. Beware especially of throwing out accusations that may put you into prison. Beware! [*He places his hand on her head*] You hate Maurice?

HENRIETTE. Beyond all bounds!

ADOLPHE. When love turns into hatred, it means that it was tainted from the start.

HENRIETTE. [*In a quieter mood*] What am I to do? Tell me, you who are the only one that understands me.

ADOLPHE. But you don't want any sermons.

HENRIETTE. Have you nothing else to offer me?

ADOLPHE. Nothing else. But they have helped me.

HENRIETTE. Preach away then!

ADOLPHE. Try to turn your hatred against yourself. Put the knife to the evil spot in yourself, for it is there that *your* trouble roots.

HENRIETTE. Explain yourself.

ADOLPHE. Part from Maurice first of all, so that you cannot nurse your qualms of conscience together. Break off your career as an artist, for the only thing that led you into it was a craving for freedom and fun—as they call it. And you have seen now how much fun there is in it. Then go home to your mother.

HENRIETTE. Never!

ADOLPHE. Some other place then.

HENRIETTE. I suppose you know, Adolphe, that I have guessed your secret and why you wouldn't accept the prize?

ADOLPHE. Oh, I assumed that you would understand a half-told story.

HENRIETTE. Well—what did you do to get peace?

ADOLPHE. What I have suggested: I became conscious of my guilt, repented, decided to turn over a new leaf, and arranged my life like that of a penitent.

HENRIETTE. How can you repent when, like me, you have no conscience? Is repentance an act of grace bestowed on you as faith is?

ADOLPHE. Everything is a grace, but it isn't granted unless you seek it— Seek!

> HENRIETTE *remains silent.*

ADOLPHE. But don't wait beyond the allotted time, or you may harden yourself until you tumble down into the irretrievable.

HENRIETTE. [*After a pause*] Is conscience fear of punishment?

ADOLPHE. No, it is the horror inspired in our better selves by the misdeeds of our lower selves.

HENRIETTE. Then I must have a conscience also?

ADOLPHE. Of course you have, but——

HENRIETTE. Tell me, Adolphe, are you what they call religious?

ADOLPHE. Not the least bit.

HENRIETTE. It's all so queer— What is religion?

ADOLPHE. Frankly speaking, I don't know! And I don't think anybody else can tell you. Sometimes it appears to me like a punishment, for nobody becomes religious without having a bad conscience.

HENRIETTE. Yes, it is a punishment. Now I know what to do. Good-bye, Adolphe!

ADOLPHE. You'll go away from here?

HENRIETTE. Yes, I am going—to where you said. Good-bye my friend! Good-bye, Madame Catherine!

MME. CATHERINE. Have you to go in such a hurry?

HENRIETTE. Yes.

ADOLPHE. Do you want me to go with you?

HENRIETTE. No, it wouldn't do. I am going alone, alone as I came here, one day in Spring, thinking that I belonged where I don't belong, and believing there was something called freedom, which does not exist. Good-bye! [*Goes out.*

MME. CATHERINE. I hope that lady never comes back, and I wish she had never come here at all!

ADOLPHE. Who knows but that she may have had some mission to fill here? And at any rate she deserves pity, endless pity.

MME. CATHERINE. I don't deny it, for all of us deserve that.

ADOLPHE. And she has even done less wrong than the rest of us.

MME. CATHERINE. That's possible, but not probable.

ADOLPHE. You are always so severe, Madame Catherine. Tell me: have you never done anything wrong?

MME. CATHERINE. [*Startled*] Of course, as I am a sinful human creature. But if you have been on thin ice and fallen in, you have a right to tell others to keep away. And you may do so without being held severe or uncharitable. Didn't I say to Monsieur Maurice the moment that lady entered here: Look out! Keep away! And he didn't, and so he fell in. Just like a naughty, self-willed child. And when a man acts like that he has to have a spanking, like any disobedient youngster.

ADOLPHE. Well, hasn't he had his spanking?

MME. CATHERINE. Yes, but it does not seem to have been enough, as he is still going around complaining.

ADOLPHE. That's a very popular interpretation of the whole intricate question.

MME. CATHERINE. Oh, pish! You do nothing but philosophise about your vices, and while you are still at it the police come along and solve the riddle. Now please leave me alone with my accounts!

ADOLPHE. There's Maurice now.

MME. CATHERINE. Yes, God bless him!

MAURICE. [*Enters, his face very flushed, and takes a seat near* ADOLPHE] Good evening.

MME. CATHERINE *nods and goes on figuring.*

ADOLPHE. Well, how's everything with you?

MAURICE. Oh, beginning to clear up.

ADOLPHE. [*Hands him a newspaper, which* MAURICE *does not take*] So you have read the paper?

MAURICE. No, I don't read the papers any longer. There's nothing but infamies in them.

ADOLPHE. But you had better read it first——

MAURICE. No, I won't! It's nothing but lies— But listen: I have found a new clue. Can you guess who committed that murder?

ADOLPHE. Nobody, nobody!

MAURICE. Do you know where Henriette was during that quarter hour when the child was left alone?— She was *there!* And it is she who has done it!

ADOLPHE. You are crazy, man.

MAURICE. Not I, but Henriette, is crazy. She suspects me and has threatened to report me.

ADOLPHE. Henriette was here a while ago, and she used the self-same words as you. Both of you are crazy, for it has been proved by a second autopsy that the child died from a well-known disease, the name of which I have forgotten.

MAURICE. It isn't true!

ADOLPHE. That's what she said also. But the official report is printed in the paper.

MAURICE. A report? Then they have made it up!

ADOLPHE. And that's also what she said. The two of you are suffering from the same mental trouble. But with her I got far enough to make her realise her own condition.

MAURICE. Where did she go?

ADOLPHE. She went far away from here to begin a new life.

MAURICE. Hm, hm!— Did you go to the funeral?

ADOLPHE. I did.

MAURICE. Well?

ADOLPHE. Well, Jeanne seemed resigned and didn't have a hard word to say about you.

MAURICE. She is a good woman.

ADOLPHE. Why did you desert her then?

MAURICE. Because I *was* crazy—blown up with pride especially—and then we had been drinking champagne——

ADOLPHE. Can you understand now why Jeanne wept when you drank champagne?

MAURICE. Yes, I understand now— And for that reason I have already written to her and asked her to forgive me— Do you think she will forgive me?

ADOLPHE. I think so, for it's not like her to hate anybody.

MAURICE. Do you think she will forgive me completely, so that she will come back to me?

ADOLPHE. Well, I don't know about *that.* You have shown yourself so poor in keeping faith that it is doubtful whether she will trust her fate to you any longer.

MAURICE. But I can feel that her fondness for me has not ceased, and I know she will come back to me.

ADOLPHE. How can you know that? How can you believe it? Didn't you even suspect her and that decent brother of hers of having sent the police after Henriette out of revenge?

MAURICE. But I don't believe it any longer—that is to say, I guess that fellow Emile is a pretty slick customer.

MME. CATHERINE. Now look here! What are you saying of Monsieur Emile? Of course, he is nothing but a workman, but if everybody kept as straight as he— There is no flaw in him, but a lot of sense and tact.

EMILE. [*Enters*] Monsieur Gérard?

MAURICE. That's me.

EMILE. Pardon me, but I have something to say to you in private.

MAURICE. Go right on. We are all friends here.

*The* ABBÉ *enters and sits down.*

EMILE. [*With a glance at the* ABBÉ] Perhaps after——

MAURICE. Never mind. The Abbé is also a friend, although he and I differ.

EMILE. You know who I am, Monsieur Gérard? My sister has asked me to give you this package as an answer to your letter.

MAURICE *takes the package and opens it.*

EMILE. And now I have only to add, seeing as I am in a way my sister's guardian, that, on her behalf as well as my own, I acknowledge you free of all obligations, now when the natural tie between you does not exist any longer.

MAURICE. But you must have a grudge against me?

EMILE. Must I? I can't see why. On the other hand, I should like to have a declaration from you, here in the presence of your friends, that you don't think either me or my sister capable of such a meanness as to send the police after Mademoiselle Henriette.

MAURICE. I wish to take back what I said, and I offer you my apology, if you will accept it.

EMILE. It is accepted. And I wish all of you a good evening. [*Goes out.*

EVERYBODY. Good evening!

MAURICE. The tie and the gloves which Jeanne gave me for the opening night of my play, and which I let Henriette throw into the fireplace. Who can have picked them up? Everything is dug up; everything comes back!— And when she gave them to me in the cemetery, she said she wanted me to look fine and handsome, so that other people would like me also— And she herself stayed at home— This hurt her too deeply, and well it might. I have no right to keep company with decent human beings. Oh, have I done this? Scoffed at a gift coming from a good heart; scorned a sacrifice offered to my own welfare. This was what I threw away in order to get—a laurel that is lying on the rubbish heap, and a bust that would have belonged in the pillory— Abbé, now I come over to you.

ABBÉ. Welcome!

MAURICE. Give me the word that I need.

ABBÉ. Do you expect me to contradict your self-accusations and inform you that you have done nothing wrong?

MAURICE. Speak the right word!

ABBÉ. With your leave, I'll say then that I have found your behaviour just as abominable as you have found it yourself.

MAURICE. What can I do, what can I do, to get out of this?

ABBÉ. You know as well as I do.

MAURICE. No, I know only that I am lost, that my life

is spoiled, my career cut off, my reputation in this world ruined forever.

ABBÉ. And so you are looking for a new existence in some better world, which you are now beginning to believe in?

MAURICE. Yes, that's it.

ABBÉ. You have been living in the flesh and you want now to live in the spirit. Are you then so sure that this world has no more attractions for you?

MAURICE. None whatever! Honour is a phantom; gold, nothing but dry leaves; women, mere intoxicants. Let me hide myself behind your consecrated walls and forget this horrible dream that has filled two days and lasted two eternities.

ABBÉ. All right! But this is not the place to go into the matter more closely. Let us make an appointment for this evening at nine o'clock in the Church of St. Germain. For I am going to preach to the inmates of St. Lazare, and that may be your first step along the hard road of penitence.

MAURICE. Penitence?

ABBÉ. Well, didn't you wish——

MAURICE. Yes, yes!

ABBÉ. Then we have vigils between midnight and two o'clock.

MAURICE. That will be splendid!

ABBÉ. Give me your hand that you will not look back.

MAURICE. [*Rising, holds out his hand*] Here is my hand, and my will goes with it.

SERVANT GIRL. [*Enters from the kitchen*] A telephone call for Monsieur Maurice.

MAURICE. From whom?

SERVANT GIRL. From the theatre.

> MAURICE *tries to get away, but the* ABBÉ *holds on to his hand.*

ABBÉ. [*To the* SERVANT GIRL] Find out what it is.

SERVANT GIRL. They want to know if Monsieur Maurice is going to attend the performance to-night.

ABBÉ. [*To* MAURICE, *who is trying to get away*] No, I won't let you go.

MAURICE. What performance is that?

ADOLPHE. Why don't you read the paper?

MME. CATHERINE *and the* ABBÉ. He hasn't read the paper?

MAURICE. It's all lies and slander. [*To the* SERVANT GIRL] Tell them that I am engaged for this evening: I am going to church.

*The* SERVANT GIRL *goes out into the kitchen.*

ADOLPHE. As you don't want to read the paper, I shall have to tell you that your play has been put on again, now when you are exonerated. And your literary friends have planned a demonstration for this evening in recognition of your indisputable talent.

MAURICE. It isn't true.

EVERYBODY. It is true.

MAURICE. [*After a pause*] I have not deserved it!

ABBÉ. Good!

ADOLPHE. And furthermore, Maurice——

MAURICE. [*Hiding his face in his hands*] Furthermore!

MME. CATHERINE. One hundred thousand francs! Do you see now that they come back to you? And the villa outside the city. Everything is coming back except Mademoiselle Henriette.

ABBÉ. [*Smiling*] You ought to take this matter a little more seriously, Madame Catherine.

MME. CATHERINE. Oh, I cannot—I just can't keep serious any longer!

[*She breaks into open laughter, which she vainly tries to smother with her handkerchief.*

ADOLPHE. Say, Maurice, the play begins at eight.

ABBÉ. But the church services are at nine.

ADOLPHE. Maurice!

MME. CATHERINE. Let us hear what the end is going to be, Monsieur Maurice.

> MAURICE *drops his head on the table, in his arms.*

ADOLPHE. Loose him, Abbé!

ABBÉ. No, it is not for me to loose or bind. He must do that himself.

MAURICE. [*Rising*] Well, I go with the Abbé.

ABBÉ. No, my young friend. I have nothing to give you but a scolding, which you can give yourself. And you owe a duty to yourself and to your good name. That you have got through with this as quickly as you have is to me a sign that you have suffered your punishment as intensely as if it had lasted an eternity. And when Providence absolves you there is nothing for me to add.

MAURICE. But why did the punishment have to be so hard when I was innocent?

ABBÉ. Hard? Only two days! And you were not innocent. For we have to stand responsible for our thoughts and words and desires also. And in your thought you became a murderer when your evil self wished the life out of your child.

MAURICE. You are right. But my decision is made. To-night I will meet you at the church in order to have a reckoning with myself—but to-morrow evening I go to the theatre.

MME. CATHERINE. A good solution, Monsieur Maurice.

ADOLPHE. Yes, that is the solution. Whew!

ABBÉ. Yes, so it is!

*Curtain.*